The Cambridge Distributed Computing System

The Cambridge Distributed Computing System

R M NEEDHAM
A J HERBERT

University of Cambridge

ADDISON-WESLEY PUBLISHING COMPANY
London · Reading, Massachusetts · Menlo Park, California
Amsterdam · Don Mills, Ontario · Manilla · Singapore
Sydney · Tokyo

Set by the authors using the Cambridge GCAL text-processing system at the Computer Laboratory, University of Cambridge.

Printed in Finland by Werner Söderström Osakeyhtiö, Member of Finnprint.

Library of Congress Cataloging in Publication Data
Needham, R. M. (Roger Michael)
The cambridge distributed computing system.

(International computer science series)
Bibliography: p.
Includes index.
1. Electronic data processing--Distributed processing.
2. University of Cambridge. I. Herbert, A. J.
(Andrew J.) 1954- . II. Title. III. Series
QA76.9.D5N5 001.64 82-1688
ISBN 0-201-14092-6 (pbk) AACR2

British Library Cataloguing in Publication Data
Needham, Roger M.
The Cambridge distributed computing system.—
(International computer science series)
1. Electronic data processing — Distributed processing
I. Title II. Herbert, Andrew J. III. Series
001.64 QA76.9.D5

ISBN 0-201-14092-6

ABCDEF 898765432

Foreword

The development during the last five years or so of wide band local communication systems is likely to have a large impact on our view of what a computer system should be. These communication systems have a bandwidth that is two or more orders of magnitude greater than that of an ordinary telephone line, while still being much less than that of an internal computer bus. The work described in this book is based on the Cambridge Digital Communication Ring, the design study for which was published in 1975. It is, however, only at the lowest levels of protocol that it matters greatly what the underlying transport system is and much of the system engineering described could equally well have been based, for example, on an Ethernet.

The ring enables services of various kinds to be put at the disposal of users connected to the ring, the most obvious being a filing service and a service for producing hard copy. In much of the work that has been reported from elsewhere, users have been provided with their own personal computers. An alternative approach is to provide a bank of centrally located computers and to allow users to attach one or more of these to their terminals and retain them for their exclusive use until they have finished with them. Work along these latter lines would appear to have progressed further in the Computer Laboratory of the University of Cambridge than it has elsewhere. The problems raised, especially those of resource management, are of much interest from a systems point of view. The authors describe a model system that they have in operation and give their views as to how further development should proceed. It is, perhaps, worth observing that the ring used to implement the system also supports other activities; for example, a user at a terminal is able to log in to one of several time-sharing systems. Similarly, a user with a personal computer could be connected to the ring and would enjoy the benefits of the services provided.

The chapter that many readers will find particularly timely is one on protection and authentication. These topics have been the subject of much debate and they take on a new aspect when seen from the standpoint of the designer of a distributed system.

Distributed computing, based on a ring or Ethernet, is a very new subject. The authors are to be commended for making available some of their experiences in book form.

Cambridge
1982

M.V. WILKES

Preface

In this book we describe and give a rationale for the distributed computing system set up in the Computer Laboratory at the University of Cambridge, England.

When the Cambridge Digital Communication Ring hardware was satisfactorily commissioned in 1976-7, it seemed the obvious thing to set up a computer system based on it and exploiting its characteristics. The main intention originally had been to promote peripheral sharing using the Ring. But with the advent of inexpensive microcomputers and the ready availability of minicomputers we were stimulated to consider the use of interconnected machines constituting a coherent system rather than just a collection. Another stimulus came as a result of experience gained by one of us (R.M.N.) when on leave in 1977 at the Xerox Palo Alto Research Center; the feeling arose that we were near the beginning of a new approach to the provision of computing facilities - a novelty comparable to that of time-sharing systems in 1963. Naturally the new opportunity ought to be embraced as energetically as the earlier one had been. We report here work that followed from 1978 to early 1982.

We would emphasise that the system is described as it is, rather than as it was meant to be, or might have been, or as it would be if done again. Hindsight has as far as possible been avoided, and where design alternatives are discussed they are the alternatives considered at the relevant time. We believe that this is the best way to present our work as a case study; the reader is invited to consider how he would have done it better, or which of our boundary conditions he would like to relax. Our main hope is that our work will be useful to other practical system designers and to those needing something concrete on which to base their teaching.

The Cambridge system as it stands is the product of many people's efforts. A list of them accompanies the bibliography; some call for particular mention here. The successful design of the Ring is due to M.V. Wilkes, D.J. Wheeler, A. Hopper and the late N.W.P. Unwin. The reliable installation and operation of a substantial Ring system owes a great deal to the careful industry of P.J. Bennett. Many pieces of hardware and software are the work of J.J. Gibbons and M.A. Johnson who is also our conscience on the propriety of protocols. The File Server was implemented by J. Dion; the TRIPOS operating system underlying the File Server and in standard use on the Processor Bank machines is the work of M. Richards and his students. The TRIPOS Filing Machine described in Chapter Seven was designed and implemented by M. Richardson. The authentication system is the work of C.G. Girling.

On another note of acknowledgement, we have learnt a great deal from friends and colleagues at Xerox PARC, where they do it differently; and the idea of writing the book was put to us one evening in The Eagle by W.D. Shepherd of the University of Strathclyde.

M.V. Wilkes was head of the Computer Laboratory when much of the work was done and encouraged the project in every possible way. The Science and Engineering Research Council contributed generously towards the support of the project.

Cambridge
1982

R.M. Needham
A.J. Herbert

Contents

1 Introduction

1.1 Background

It is well known that the dramatic developments of the last few years in integrated circuit technology have revolutionised the approach taken to the provision of computer hardware. The use of many microcomputers with substantial amounts of memory is considered routine, and it is quite reasonable to use machines for a single function only. The exploitation of this possibility in the cause of simplicity has been made much easier by another development, perhaps less well known, in communication technology. It is now possible to interconnect computers in a building or a cluster of buildings by means of a **local area network.** Such networks typically carry data at rates from a megabit per second upwards with very high reliability. Both in terms of speed and of reliability, they may be contrasted with earlier systems using telephone lines. In traditional networks much effort had to be devoted to protocols that made the best use possible of the limited bandwidth and that were as rugged as possible against the effects of transmission error. Connection equipment tended to be expensive, and accordingly there was good reason to minimise the number of systems connected. The modern local network is capable of being interfaced much more cheaply and of being used with much simpler protocols. It is not nearly so necessary to optimise the use of its bandwidth, because there is so much at hand and because the network cost has not been perceptibly increased to provide that bandwidth.

The conjunction of the two developments has led to a particular style of **distributed computing** in which the work of a system is performed by a collection of computers connected via a network. The objective is to make use if possible of the low cost of individual processing elements to obtain high performance through the use of many of them. The use of many processors may be approached through tight coupling, in which processors typically share some or all of their memory and cooperate closely in the execution of parallel algorithms. This approach exploits the developments in microelectronics but not those in communication. The alternative approach depends on loose coupling and functional dedication. Machines are used for particular purposes and are placed where appropriate for that purpose, being scattered according to need through an office, factory, or laboratory complex. It is this style of distributed computing that forms the topic of the present book; the experience recorded here concerns the design and development of the structures necessary for the reliable and harmonious cooperation of diverse systems. The goal is to strike a balance between unity and diversity. There should be sufficient unity of approach to make it easy for machines to cooperate and to make it easy to design and install new services; there should not be constraints enforced by convention or hardware that make it impossible to provide a particular service in a satisfactory way.

This book describes the results of a project developed in this spirit and directed towards the particular goal of providing the kind of services one expects from a time-sharing system based on a substantial mainframe. In such an environment each user has a terminal connected to a central machine; it being typical that only a small proportion of the whole user community is active at once. There are important advantages to this approach. The entire user community can benefit from the work of individuals since there are no unnecessary barriers to the sharing of useful programs, results, or data. It is further guaranteed that all users are able to work in a common environment so that there is a certain coherence about the programs they develop. These aspects result from what might be called benign sharing. Unfortunately there are drawbacks too. The performance of the system as perceived by a user is dependent on the number of other users active at a time; the detail of the dependence is unknown and the performance is thus unpredictable. Much research in operating systems has been directed to balancing performance and making it more predictable, but it cannot be said to have been wholly successful. A second drawback is the vulnerability of the system to failures of single components. The single processor is a weak point both in respect of hardware failures and of software-induced crashes.

In the Cambridge Distributed System described here, the central mainframe is replaced by a collection of smaller computers allocated individually to users. The administration of the allocation functions is reminiscent of parts of an operating system for a central machine; in the Distributed System small computers are assigned (statically) to the various administrative tasks. It is found convenient to use a number of machines for this purpose rather than just one for reasons of performance, flexibility, and resilience. Performance is much more predictable when different administrative functions are not competing for machine cycles with each other or with applications; the allocation of individual machines makes development and software enhancement much easier; finally it is much more likely that a distributed system will survive partial failure. An advantage of distributed systems that applies both to the administrative machines and the application machines is that hardware enhancement is very easy. If more total power is needed, one simply adds more application machines. If the administrative system becomes overloaded, one subdivides the functions and adds more administrative machines.

The remainder of this chapter surveys the general approaches used in the class of distributed systems of which the Cambridge Distributed System is an example.

Systems of this type depend upon the use of local area networks, which are discussed in general terms in Chapter Three. The present system uses the **Cambridge Digital Communication Ring**, developed in the Computer Laboratory. From the point of view of the system architect, however, the precise choice of local network technology is not of great significance since several such systems offer very similar facilities.

1.2 Servers

One of the most straightforward applications of local networks is to interconnect machines that would otherwise be viable, self-contained systems, each with its own disc, keyboard, display and perhaps hard copy device. The network is used to transfer files from the filing system of one machine to the filing system of another as an aid to cooperation and software distribution, but occupies an ancillary rather than a central place in the overall system. As such a design is modified in the interest of flexibility and economy, the network comes to play a much more central role.

All the machines in a scheme of the sort just mentioned will have common requirements, such as the need to produce hard copy documents. Even if it is economically feasible to provide some sort of hard copy facility for each machine it is certainly not a viable proposition to provide good quality hard copy facilities in large numbers. The cost would be excessive, the maintenance commitment unsupportable, and the utilisation minimal. The obvious alternative is to provide a suitable number of printers attached to the network so as to be conveniently available to the users of the several computers. Such printers, or, more accurately, the computers that control them, are examples of **servers**, placed in order to provide services upon request. Another example is that of a **file server**, a machine supplied with extensive disc storage for holding files on behalf of a number of users. There are substantial economies of scale in the provision of disc storage, and there are also attractions in minimising the number of distinct electromechanical devices used, since they are noisy and need maintenance.

The influence of the use of servers on the general shape of the system is substantial, going far beyond the financial benefits already alluded to. As soon as facilities that are necessary for most computation are provided in this way, the individual computers become much less autonomous and the network much more important. Not much can be done without filing and printing, for example, and the absence or inaccessibility of these services is almost as bad as not having a computer at all. In addition, there are advantages to a certain uniformity of service: for example a uniform way of indicating on output the identity of the user on whose behalf it is printed, or a uniform way of archiving and backup for files. Circumstances alter cases, and it would be foolish to attempt an universal judgement on whether it is worthwhile to accept a loss of autarky in return for centrally organised services. In designing a system it should not be necessary to pose the sharp question, because the provision of one or more file servers does not preclude the attachment of a substantial disc to an ordinary computer.

Servers should thus be thought of as providing additions or enrichments to the environment in which programs operate: a function reminiscent of that of the components of an operating system for a shared machine. Indeed, many of the design considerations for servers are indistinguishable from those for traditional operating systems - though the analogy should not be pressed too far. One of the motives for the development of distributed systems is precisely to get away from the rigid and often over-structured environment of the shared machine, and it would be a serious error to regenerate that environment by imposing too much structure in the distributed case. Fortunately, the use of a server is voluntary in a sense that the use of an operating system facility in a shared machine is usually not. It is not difficult, in principle, to add a new printing server in a distributed system, the new server having a quite different interface from older ones. "The management" may well not even need to know.

Servers need not be associated with the control of physical devices. When the machines connected to a network form part of a coherent system, as in our case, there are a number of management tasks to be carried out and these may be assigned to servers in a similar way to the control of devices. Typical examples include authentication, access control, and message distribution. In Chapter Two, an overview of the Cambridge Distributed System, the functions of a number of essential management servers will be outlined.

Another aspect of the general approach using servers is a resulting tolerance to certain partial failures. If services reside in different computers then the failure of one machine will not necessarily affect the others, even if the system as a whole performs at a reduced level. Replication of services in the interest of robustness is easy; although little deliberate effort in this direction has been made in our experimental work it is evident from experience of the Cambridge System in use that the effect is present.

1.3 Personal computers

It is the conventional wisdom that users are better served by the provision of personal computers used exclusively by individuals rather than by giving them access to a time-sharing system. It is also becoming much more practical to proceed in this manner as the price of computer hardware falls. In the sort of environment where every user had a terminal in the past, every user can now have a computer. The nature and purpose of operating systems change radically in a personal computer environment. They are no longer there to maximise throughput but to maximise convenience, and it is possible to design them more readily now that they do not have to serve conflicting purposes.

The benefits of personal computers are obvious; they are always to hand, dedicated to the user and under his control. Many users of time-shared computers find more traditional approaches to be lacking in precisely these respects. Ranking high in the demonology of habitual computer users are managerial decisions as to whether a service should be available at a particular time or not, insistence on the use of particular software environments, and, perhaps most of all, inability to predict how long a computation will take. A less well-known advantage, which may account for some of the popularity of personal computers with senior people, is that the user can fumble and make blunders in decent privacy. In isolation, however, there are some disadvantages to personal machines. Cooperation between people working on the same project is difficult and the propagation of useful software awkward. These drawbacks are readily overcome by connecting the personal machines together by means of a local network; material may then be moved between machines, and servers may be exploited in the ways mentioned above. As soon as this step is taken, though, the use of servers has removed some of the autarky desired by the personal computer user.

The conventional image of a system based upon personal computers and local area networks is that of a machine of modest size complete with keyboard and display in every office. The machines are typically small enough in physical dimensions to fit unobtrusively in an office. At one end of the scale there are desk-top computers that may even be integrated into the display. These small machines however are of very limited capability; for example they may be suitable for reading electronic mail and editing files, but they cannot support major applications such as databases, computer-aided design systems and heavy numerical computation. These applications may quite easily outgrow even more substantial personal computers. As the speed and memory capacity of a computer system grows there are other increases beyond just physical dimensions. High-speed circuitry may require cooling; powerful fans blowing air through the machine will make it too noisy for the office environment.

The direct assignment of computers to users can be inflexible in two respects. The first relates to variations in a user's requirements. For much of the time a user editing programs and compiling them does not require the services of a large machine. However from time to time he may wish to run a package that needs a powerful computer. It is clearly tedious if he has to leave his office to run the package; yet, at the same time, it is hard to justify giving him exclusive use of the bigger computer all of the time. The second form of inflexibility is an extension of this with respect to running distributed algorithms. Some computations can be speeded up by spreading them over several machines running together. Clearly it would be nonsensical to fill a user's office with numerous machines to this effect. It would be better if there was some systematic way of locating other machines that are not being used and exercising the same control over them as is available over the machine in the user's office.

In the context of an office it makes practical sense to assign a machine to each individual if that person's job is dependent upon the use of a computer. There are other situations where such an assignment is not appropriate; for example in an organization that comprises a large potential user community of which only some proportion needs to be computing simultaneously. A typical example here would be the central computing service in a university or research establishment. It is clearly not economically reasonable to give every user a private machine in his office in this situation. Furthermore, in this sort of environment it is common for the computing needs of the active users to be beyond the capabilities of an office-based computer system. It is to the resolution of the conflicts in the use of personal computers that the Cambridge Distributed System is directed.

1.4 The Cambridge approach

In the Cambridge Distributed System each user has a private terminal that contains an integral personal computer of modest capabilities. This personal machine is only capable of minor duties. One of these includes the ability to connect as a remote terminal to some other machine on the network. The bulk of the computing power in the system rests with a collective of more powerful computers known as the **Processor Bank.** Processor Bank machines are not committed to any particular user.

When a user wishes to engage in work that is too demanding for his personal machine, he may approach the system with a request for a machine. If one of suitable characteristics is free, it is allocated exclusively to the user for as long as he wishes to use it. His local computer acts as a remote terminal to the allocated machine. Thus the machines in the Processor Bank may be thought of as **processing servers** since they are provided by the system to supply computing power to users.

A processing server cannot have local discs because it will be allocated to different users upon demand. Instead reliance is placed upon a central file server for storing users' permanent data. The file server can be accessed by any machine and, in consequence, a user can get hold of files independently of the identity of the allocated machine.

Mechanisms are provided so that the temporary owner of a processing server has at least the same degree of control over the machine as would be available if the machines control panel was physically accessible to its owner. Users can load different binary programs into their machines at any time during a session of use and operations for debugging at the hardware level are provided. Since the necessary operations are in fact provided by software services there is scope for providing a richer range of functions and automation than is possible ordinarily. There are no restrictions placed upon the code that can be loaded into a processing server. Users are free to write their own operating systems and packages taking advantage of the various services available on the network. The freedom from arbitrary constraints upon programs is an important aspect of personal computing.

In the same way that a time-sharing system allocates and controls the use of computing resources, the Cambridge Distributed System has facilities for exercising control over the allocation of processing servers. However, once a user has gained use of a machine, he may reap all of the benefits of personal computing in terms of performance and control. Rather than sharing the cycles of a mainframe, the user is sharing a collection of machines. Clearly, it is necessary that the Processor Bank be sufficiently well endowed with computers to support the expected demand. In practical terms this will amount to a slight over supply of machines, but with the present trends to ever cheaper hardware this is a small price to pay in return for the benefits.

The Processor Bank is well placed for dealing with a heterogeous collection of machines: a typical system might contain a majority of one type of machine that is suitable for most users' needs, together with smaller numbers of machines for users with greater demands. It is a straightforward procedure to handle distributed computations since the allocation of several machines to one user is a simple extension to the basic machinery.

The processing servers rely on numerous other services to provide operating system like functions. There are also services concerned with the allocation and organization of the Processor Bank. The server philosophy is taken to an extreme by assigning each service to its own server computer. This approach is clearly dependent upon the availability of inexpensive computers to act as the servers and also upon the low cost of connecting simple machines to the network. The approach is one of functional distribution of services. The services are truly independent: the interfaces between them are defined in terms of communication protocols for exchanging data over the network. Since each service runs in a dedicated machine, there are no problems of interference as there could be if several of them had to be supported by a single machine. The level of operating system support needed by services is modest, because a single simple program has only limited needs for concurrency and memory management. In particular, there is not the problem of protecting the program of one service from erroneous execution by another program in the same machine, nor is there the problem of scheduling between a number of competing services.

The Cambridge Distributed System is capable of interworking with the other ways of using local area networks described in the previous section. Mainframe computers can be integrated into the system, using the mechanisms for remote terminal access to connect users terminals to the mainframe. The terminal in this case may be a personal computer acting as an intelligent terminal, or it may be a more ordinary terminal attached to a terminal concentrator. The mainframe may choose to use the services of the network to a greater or lesser extent. For example, the mainframe may have a private filing system on its own discs rather than use a file server, but on the other hand it may direct output to a printing server. Similar remarks apply to the user who owns a powerful personal computer.

It is easy to arrange that users who have access to ordinary terminals as opposed to computers can be integrated into the system. All that is required is a service on the network that is capable of acting as a place holder for a user while he seeks a processing server to support all of his computing. Once a processing server is allocated, the terminal connection can be routed directly to the processing server and disengaged from the intermediary service.

1.5 Implementation

In the preceding paragraphs, the overall architecture of the Cambridge Distributed System has been presented. The rest of this book is a description of the implementation of the system. The next chapter surveys the principal components of the implementation from the point of view of a user. Succeeding chapters look at particular aspects of the system in greater detail, explaining the underlying mechanisms.

12 Cambridge distributed system

To build a full-scale version of the system was beyond the resources of the Computer Laboratory. Instead a pilot model system was implemented to investigate the important aspects of the overall design. In the model system the Processor Bank consists of about fifteen minicomputers sufficient to run single user operating systems and meet the needs of the research community for development and extension of the system. The system is also used as a general computing service by other groups in the Laboratory.

Users have access to ordinary screen-based terminals connected to terminal concentrators. There are a number of larger machines which can be accessed across the network for terminal sessions, job submission and file transfer. The only major aspect of the total design that is absent in the model system is that of the user with a personal machine who only makes intermittent use of the Processor Bank. Apart from this omission, the model implementation is faithful to the guiding plan and is a useful computer system in its own right.

The work reported here represents the state of the distributed system in early 1982 when some fifty machines of one sort or another are connected together. Development continues within the general approach of allocating computers from a central pool on demand.

2 Overview

2.1 At the terminal

The first point of contact between the ordinary user and the system is the **Terminal Concentrator** to which the user's terminal is connected. Initially the user is talking to a simple monitor program within the concentrator. This program organizes the connection of the terminal to computers on the network. At any time in the course of a session the user may press the 'break' key on the terminal to get the attention of the monitor program. This enables him to run several connections from the terminal at once; there are monitor commands to select which stream has control over the screen and keyboard. The screen can be made exclusive to just one connection, or output from several can be interleaved under the user's control. An appropriate command in the monitor sends a break signal to a host computer. From the monitor it is possible to close both individual connections and the complete set. This gives the facility for disconnecting from a machine even if for some unfortunate reason the machine is ignoring commands from the user.

To the host computer, the terminal concentrator offers a variety of services. It is possible for the concentrator to act in a transparent mode where every key stroke is sent to the host which must then deal with echoing it back. This mode is most appropriate for programs such as screen-based editors, where individual key strokes often result in significant changes to the data being displayed. The other mode of operation of the terminal concentrator is that in which it assembles complete lines of text and echoes them locally. In this mode there are a number of editing functions built in for erasing mistyped characters or lines. This style of operation is suited to simple-minded programs with a record or line orientated view of input. There are a number of advantages in processing lines locally in the concentrator. One is that of uniformity; the same editing conventions apply independently of the host to which a connection is made. Another advantage is efficiency; the host is spared from the task of low-level character handling. This is particularly helpful when the host is a small microcomputer, where the overheads of character handling would be a nuisance.

2.2 Getting started

The user who wants access to a machine from the Processor Bank has first to connect to a group of network services that organize the allocation of machines. At the heart of the group is the **Resource Manager**. It is responsible for knowing which machines are allocated, to whom, and for how long. Additionally, it causes allocated machines to be loaded with the program or operating system required by the user. Commands are sent to the Resource Manager specifying a user's requirements in terms of the identity of the system to be loaded, how long it is wanted and the sort of machine needed. The latter is described as a series of attributes, some of which are very general, such as the generic type of machine, whereas others are more particular, perhaps demanding a machine with a large memory configuration or faster processor. Machines can be retained up to the maximum time declared at the time of allocation. If a machine is not returned to the Resource Manager before this time limit is over, the Resource Manager will automatically regain control over it. To simplify matters for the ordinary user the Resource Manager knows the description and sensible default times and attributes for a number of commonly used systems. In this case the user simply asks for the system by name and the Resource Manager seeks out in its internal tables a configuration of the system that will be suited to one of the currently free processing servers.

The interface to the Resource Manager is a low-level Ring protocol so that requests to it can be made by other computers to establish multi-machine computations. For the user at a terminal there is a service known as the **Session Manager** that provides a user level interface to the Resource Manager. Initially the user connects his terminal to the Session Manager and then gives commands which are translated by the Session Manager into low-level requests to the Resource Manager. Once the Resource Manager has caused a machine to be allocated and loaded, the Session Manager hands the terminal connection over to the newly allocated personal computer. Anything typed subsequently by the user is passed on by the terminal concentrator directly to the personal computer. To simplify matters further, the Session Manager service has a number of aliases: if a user connects to it using such an alias, the Session Manager will implicitly obey the necessary commands to get the system conventionally associated with the alias. For most users this is the standard way of getting started and appears to be very similar to logging in to a time-sharing system: the user nominates the system he wants, there is a short pause and then the connection is established.

2.3 Using a processing server

The most common use made of the Processor Bank is that of running simple single user operating systems. Since a processing server has no discs of its own, the operating system is dependent upon the **File Server** for permanent storage of data. If it had been the case that only one system made use of the File Server, it would have been sensible to make the File Server responsible for all aspects of the filing system including naming and access control. However, there are a number of operating systems that utilise the File

Server, each with noticeably different designs of filing system. Furthermore, the File Server is also used as permanent data storage by several servers, although not within a context that can be justifiably described as a 'filing system'. For all of these reasons, it was decided to build a universal file server. That is to say one that provides a set of facilities sufficient to support many different styles of filing system, without imposing constraints on any of them. Thus, for example, the File Server deals with issues such as disc space management, integrity, atomic update of data and interlocks on access to shared files. The File Server provides a basic naming substrate and the client systems are left to mould this into the particular model of a filing system they wish to present to users. The naming of files is such that it is impossible for an arbitrary user to access the files of another, unless explicitly permitted to do so by the higher level filing system. Thus the different filing systems are protected from one another.

When an operating system is loaded into a processing server a check is made on the identity of the user before permitting him use of its filing system. This is necessary as a protection against illegal access. To effect this purpose a network-wide authentication system is provided. In return for presenting the correct password, the User Authentication Server will yield a token which can be offered to other services as proof of identity. Tokens are simply 64 bit strings with a random component so that it is hard to forge them, or guess them. The tokens are used as a sort of temporary password and only persist while the user remains logged in. When he comes to log in again a new token is issued. Thus the short lifetime of these tokens makes them a safer proof of identity than would be the case if textual passwords were continuously passed over the network. The mechanisms underlying the authentication server are quite general and can be used to authenticate the use of privileges, or the right of access to a particular class of resources in addition to the simple recognition of users by password.

Apart from the realization that he has a machine entirely to himself, the user of the Processor Bank need not be aware that he is working in a distributed environment. The operating system he uses may care to conceal the fact. There are occasions when the difference does become apparent and that is when one of the servers used by the operating system is not available for any reason. In these cases, the operating system can either warn the user or take sensible default action. For example, if the Printer Server is busy when a print command is given, the document could be spooled locally until the server is free. There are more severe conditions where nothing can be done; if the File Server is broken, most systems become impotent. One of the challenges of working in a distributed environment is to design systems where the user interface is sufficiently well-designed that the user does not have to possess an image of the total system in order make sense of the behaviour of his own machine.

One respect in which a processing server is unusual is in its connection to the Ring. Since the machine is dependent upon the Ring for all services, the connection must be efficient and offer high throughput. Furthermore, the interface to the Ring is the only point at which control can be exercised over a processing server because of the design policy that the processing server itself is at the total disposal of the user. Thus loading systems, stopping and starting execution are all the responsibility of the Ring interface. In fact processing servers have an interface to the Ring controlled by a high-speed microcomputer. It deals with the issues of getting a machine loaded and provides a DMA interface for data transfer across the Ring. The interface is not sufficiently powerful to be able to cope with fetching memory images from the File Server and unpicking a complicated loading format. Instead this is left to a server called the **Ancilla**. The Ancilla receives orders from the Resource Manager to load particular machines. It sets about transferring data from the File Server, converting it to the primitive format expected by a processing server Ring interface. The Ancilla is also responsible for hiding any low-level details about the loading protocol in the Ring interface of a particular variety of machine - thereby offering a uniform set of operations at the higher level.

The Resource Manager and Ancilla working together are in a position to provide the user with help when debugging on a bare machine. A new copy of a program can be loaded into a previously allocated machine on behalf of its owner in the event of a catastrophic failure. The Ancilla has the ability to set a debugging mode in processing server Ring interfaces. The interface is given the identity of a debugging machine and allows it to read and write memory locations arbitrarily. These facilities can be built upon to provide a range of debugging tools from simple post-mortem dumping to full scale interactive systems. It is the general aim of the Resource Manager and Ancilla services that a user should have as much, if not more, control over a machine as he would if its control panel was in his office.

When a user has finished with a machine, or when the time limit on a session expires, it is left to the Resource Manager to tidy up. Any outstanding debugging sessions have to be cancelled and a null program is loaded into the machine to inhibit it from further action.

2.4 The small servers

The correct working of the system at user level is clearly dependent upon a collection of network services such as the Resource Manager, Session Manager, Ancilla and others. All of these services run in small microcomputers with each machine responsible for just one service. The servers are designed to run unattended and to restart automatically after loss of power and other transient forms of disconnection. This level of management is divided between a small control program common to all of the small servers and a special server called the **Boot Server**. When a small server is turned on, a forced entry is made to the control program. Its first act is to send a message across the Ring to the Boot Server asking to be loaded with the correct program. The Boot Server recognises such requests and replies by sending back a simple memory image of the appropriate code for the server. The control program then branches into the loaded code and the service is alive.

Clearly the Boot Server has a special position in the overall system and must not depend upon any of the other servers for its own operation. In the present system, the Boot Server runs on a free-standing computer with its own local discs. If remote login is not possible because of a Ring disruption, the various files and tables held by the server can all be manipulated by logging in at dedicated terminals attached directly to it. (Terminal concentrators, along with all of the other servers driving peripherals, are also examples of small servers.) It is essential that some level of recovery should be possible should the Boot Server fail. If the small server control program cannot solicit a reply from the Boot Server, it enters a special mode in which any machine can mimic the loading protocol and insert code into the server. This allows manual intervention to restart a service in the absence of the Boot Server. To cope with temporary loss of the Boot Server, the control program will cycle alternately between polling the Boot Server and taking a response from any machine. Thus if the Boot Server recovers, the normal automatic mechanisms will come into play.

The microcomputers used to support the network services are comparatively feeble in terms of computing power and memory capacity. From the point of view of the services this is not a problem, since they are mostly simple programs and undemanding. Because of their simplicity, the servers are inexpensive to construct and the assignment of individual machines to services is not an unjustifiable luxury.

For the systems programmer wishing to write and install a new service, however, there are difficulties to be faced. The microcomputer systems are not capable of supporting a filing system or running compilers, editors and other user software. Instead, program development must be done elsewhere, usually on a processing server. There are various cross assemblers and compilers to generate object code for loading into servers. For software development and testing there are a number of uncommitted small server systems attached to the Ring. When an uncommitted system is started the Boot Server loads a simple bootstrap program that waits for object code to be sent from any machine on the Ring. Thus a systems programmer can test new code in one of the free machines. As part of the loading protocol a debugging connection between the small server and the programmer's machine is set up. The connection directs debugging commands from the user to the small server's control program. The facilities provided are rudimentary, but can be easily extended by a debugging stub in the small server, driven by the user's debugging program to provide high level operations such as breakpoints, memory dumping and examining machine registers. To complete the suite of debugging functions, it is possible for the programmer to generate a restart signal in order to completely reload a machine. The culmination of all these measures is that a systems programmer can work on a new service from the terminal in his office without the need to have physical access to the microcomputer system being used. Obviously, in the case of a machine driving a peripheral device, it is likely that for some of the time at least the programmer will need to be close to the device so that it can be observed. Even so, he gains the advantage of his programming environment running on a more powerful machine from the Processor Bank.

A service is normally only installed fully in the Boot Server and allocated a dedicated machine after it has been thoroughly tested in the environment described above. However there are occasions when a trusted service may encounter a previously unnoticed bug and crash. The small server control program is entered automatically in the event of several hardware detected errors such as stack overflow, or fetching instructions from uninitialised memory. First a record of the crash is sent to a server, called the **Logger**, which prints the information on a teletypewriter. The record is timestamped, taking the time from another server, the **Time Server**, which monitors clock transmissions sent by radio. Once the event has been noted, the small server is restarted in the normal way. There are certain defensive measures that will take a server out of use if it fails repeatedly, as might occur because of a hardware fault.

To the ordinary user, the small server system is entirely self-sustaining; restarting and dealing with errors are handled automatically. Because they are very simple circuits, the servers are in practice extremely reliable and operating systems can make use of them safely. Taken in unison the collection of services amounts to a network-wide operating system.

2.5 The Name Server

To use any of the various services it is essential to have the ability to address them. If the system was entirely static all services could be known by their location on the Ring and a directory of Ring addresses (i.e. numbers) could be published. In a changing environment this is too inflexible: services are often moved from one machine to another and machines may be moved to new positions on the network. To cope with these changes, services are located by looking up a textual name for the service in a special **Name Server**. This machine is special in that its location on the Ring is fixed for all time and well-known. To find out where a service is currently located a simple message exchange with the Name Server will translate a textual service name into a numeric Ring address. From the point of view of system management, the Name Server is a central register of services and machines; any relocation in either category becomes public simply by changing the Name Server's tables. To the user, the use of textual names makes it easier to remember about services because they can be given mnemonic names which do not change. It is very unusual for a user to know the low-level addresses into which names are turned. As an example of the Name Server in operation, when the connect command is given to a terminal concentrator monitor, the command includes the textual name of the system required. A standard prefix denoting remote terminal access is joined onto the front of the system name and the whole looked up in the Name Server. This yields a Ring address to which the concentrator should open a remote terminal stream. The Session Manager, which deals with terminal connection into the Processor Bank, has a number of names corresponding to a variety of commonly used systems. Each name turns into a different address which is distinguished internally by the Session Manager, and the appropriate Resource Manager commands are generated automatically.

2.6 Other services

Within the Cambridge Distributed System several other free standing machines are included with their own fixed operating systems. The most notable is the CAP Computer, built as part of an earlier research project. The CAP runs a time-sharing service for a number of users concurrently. However, CAP has no peripheral devices of its own: the File Server is used for both filing system and swapping purposes, terminals are connected from across the Ring and printing is done using the Printer Server. CAP users are in general terms not aware that so much of the operating system is dependent upon the network.

The University of Cambridge Data Network is connected to the Ring. It provides terminal and remote job entry facilities into a central mainframe and also to other machines on various national telecommunication networks. It is also possible to do file transfers between the machines in the Cambridge Distributed System and the central service mainframe.

2.7 Detailed description

Succeeding chapters deal in greater detail with the programs and protocols at the basis of the system overviewed here. Chapter Three deals with the particular properties of the Ring and the influence of high bandwidth communications on systems and protocols. Chapter Four looks at the design requirements of file servers and how they can be met. It contains an account of the operations and implementation of the File Server at Cambridge. Chapter Five deals with the control and debugging of small servers. Chapter Six lists the various simple services available to users. Chapters Seven and Eight are concerned with the Processor Bank. Chapter Seven looks at the processing servers and their capabilities; Chapter Eight describes the management and control of the Processor Bank as a whole. Chapter Nine explains how the various protection and authentication problems in the system are tackled.

The Cambridge Digital Communication Ring

3.1 Local area networks

The Cambridge Digital Communication Ring has particular properties that need to be understood in order to follow the work described in this book. It also shares those properties of local communication systems that set them apart as a class from wide area networks and affect the style in which they are used. It is therefore appropriate to start with a brief outline of the relevant properties of local networks in general.

Local networks are characterised firstly by speed. Rates vary, and one has to be careful to distinguish between network capacity and point-to-point bandwidth; however, it is reasonable to say that, in a local network, the relevant numbers are quoted in megabits/second. One consequence is that, by and large, availability of bandwidth is not really an issue. Practical local area networks are never heavily loaded and are designed under this assumption. When supporting applications such as the Cambridge Distributed Computing System, observation shows typical utilisations of 10-30% during a busy second. The limitations on the rate of data transfer between machines come from the behaviour of the machines themselves - such as from the overheads involved in task-switching, in copying data from buffer to buffer, and in sending acknowledgements. It is thus important to plan the programs used in the various machines to be sufficiently simple so that they can exploit the bandwidth fully. In older communication systems, by contrast, the accent was on communicating as little as possible because of the limited bandwidth available when using conventional telecommunications equipment.

Secondly, local networks are not very prone to error. Rates of corruption of bits of one in 10^{10} or one in 10^{11} are common. A desirable simplicity of protocol results because a good deal of material may be transmitted before checking for satisfactory receipt. Since low level error control is one of the major sources of protocol overhead, the low error rate is very beneficial.

Finally local networks are often, if not invariably, sequential. Material sent over them may be lost but it will not become disordered. The practical effect of this is that it is considered perfectly reasonable to send a quantity of data with the assertion that if the right quantity arrives in correct-looking packets then it was the right data. The network might lose data but it certainly will not invent it.

All of these properties are very different from those of wide area networks, and have a profound effect on the style in which local networks are used. Calling on other machines for trivial services can be done at any time; it is possible to consider relying on very high level recovery action in the event of communication failures because they happen so rarely. A large number of architectures have been proposed, a considerable number implemented, and extensive practical experience is available for several of them. The most common architectures are contention buses, token rings, and empty slot rings.

The best known contention bus is the Xerox **Ethernet.** An Ethernet consists of a single length of co-axial cable forming a passive bus interconnecting a number of **taps** that provide the points to which devices can be connected. Ethernets are intrinsically broadcast mediums; information sent out by one station goes to all stations on the bus. Data is normally transmitted in bursts called **packets** and each packet is labelled with its intended destination. It is left to individual stations to recognise and filter off packets for the device they connect. An Ethernet station transmits only when the bus appears quiet.

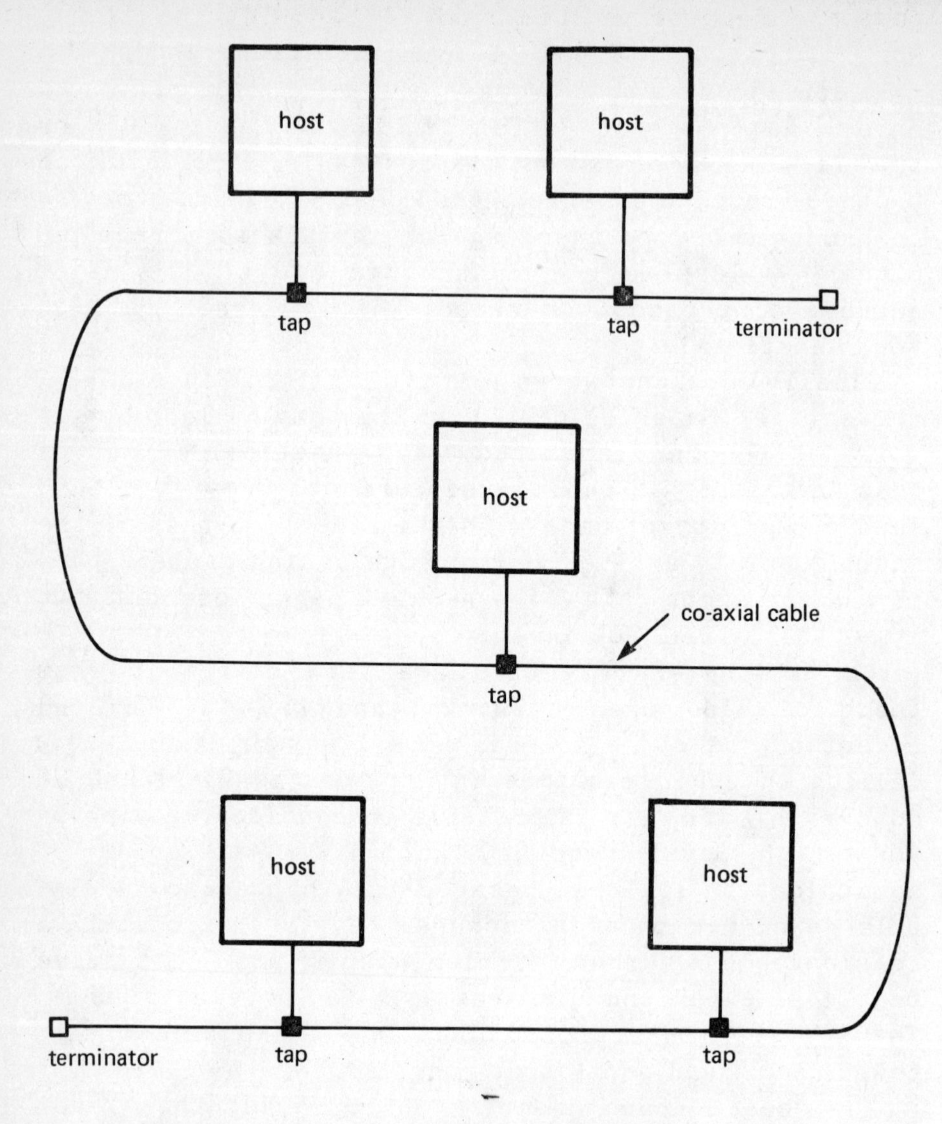

A Typical Ethernet System

During transmission a watch is kept to see whether another station begins transmitting too; if such a collision occurs then both stations abandon their transmissions and each pause for a random delay before attempting to retransmit. It is this behaviour that gives rise to use of the term contention because, unlike some of the other architectures, there is no orderly discipline for accessing the bus. A reasonable analogy is that of a meeting of polite people without a chairman.

Token rings have all stations connected in a loop around which a special signal called the **token** circulates. To transmit, a station must wait until it is able to remove the token, whereupon it is allowed to send data onto the loop. Once the transmission is complete the station should establish the token signal once more to indicate that the loop is free. Thus the circulation of the token establishes an orderly discipline for accessing the loop so that at most one station is transmitting at any time. It is rather like a meeting with only one microphone (presumed necessary for communication) passed from hand to hand.

An **empty slot ring** circulates an endless train of **slots** or packet frames of fixed size. These slots are typically very much smaller than the size of packets transmitted on Ethernets and token rings since the bits comprising the train must be stored in the ring. To transmit, a station awaits an empty slot and fills it. Each station monitors passing slots, and intercepts filled slots containing data destined to it. Various rules may be adopted for emptying the slot after its contents have been received. Thus, unlike Ethernets and token rings, the bandwidth of an empty slot ring can be shared between as many transmitters as there are slots on the ring. The point-to-point bandwidth is only some part of the bandwidth of the transmission medium. But, in contrast to the other two architectures, the latency of access to the medium is greatly reduced, provided that steps are taken to avoid particular stations hogging slots. An empty slot ring is not like any kind of meeting; physical analogies are possible with rollercoasters and other fairground equipment, or with paternoster lifts.

All three types of local network have energetic and variously moneyed advocates; for the purposes of applications such as the Cambridge Distributed System (though not for all imaginable purposes), they are almost indistinguishable in practice.

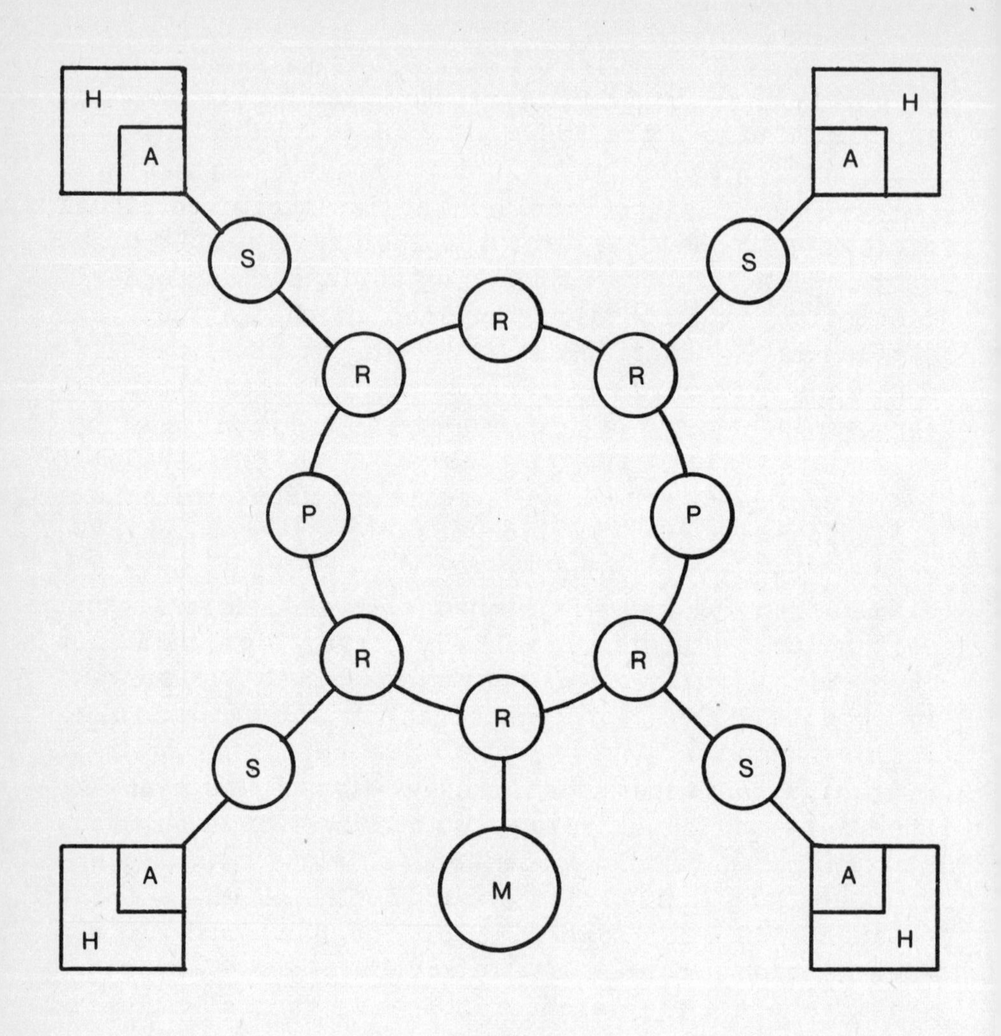

R Repeaters
S Stations
A Access Circuits
H Host Computers
M Monitor Station
P Power Supplies

A Typical Cambridge Ring

3.2 The Cambridge Ring

This section describes the Cambridge Ring at a system level; engineering aspects are to be found in other publications mentioned in the Bibliography. It should be emphasised that what is described here is the Ring that has been used for the experimental work in Distributed Computing which is the principal subject of this book. Later Rings developed in Cambridge and some of the commercial products based on the Cambridge design differ in detail.

The Cambridge Ring is an empty slot ring with a raw data rate of 10 megabits/second. Transmission is usually over dual twisted-pairs[1] used for ordinary telephone cable. However, since the Ring is a point-to-point system, it is not necessary to use the same medium throughout an installation, and fibre optic or co-axial cable may be substituted where a long link is needed. The most basic piece of Ring apparatus is the **repeater**, which is required wherever any device is attached and also where signal regeneration is needed. A repeater not only passes the bit stream to its output; the data are also passed out of the repeater for external inspection, and, if the repeater is suitably enabled, external data may be substituted for the incoming bit stream. The repeaters draw their power from the Ring itself so that the integrity of the Ring does not depend on all connected devices being switched on.

Data is transmitted round the Ring in **minipackets**. Each minipacket consists of two data bytes, a source address byte, a destination address byte, two response bits and four control bits as shown below. A constant number of slots circulate round the Ring, the number being determined by the length of wire and the number of repeaters. Each slot is able to contain one minipacket. It is required that there is at least one bit time of gap to locate the beginning and end of the

---

[1] Twisted pairs produce radiation, and although this is not a problem on the original site, it may easily be avoided by shielding.

packet train. If there were 122 bits altogether in the Ring there would then be three slots in the train with an eight bit gap. It should be emphasised that the number of slots is likely to be small. The Ring in use at the time of writing for the distributed system is about a kilometer long, and has over fifty devices connected. It has four slots and a short gap, and is by far the largest Cambridge Ring in use.

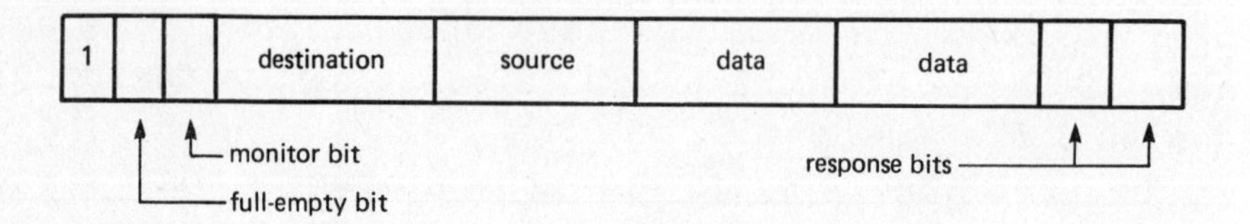

Wherever a device is to be connected to a repeater it is necessary to insert a **station.** A station has an eight bit address set on a coding plug which is associated with each minipacket sent and determines to which incoming minipackets the station will respond. Each station has a register which may be used to permit reception from any source, from a nominated source, or from no source. Stations are powered by the device they attach, not by the Ring. It is not necessary for the Ring's integrity that stations be powered at all. The station unit watches the bit stream emitted by the repeater and detects the framing of the minipackets. To transmit a minipacket it is necessary to load into the station the data bytes and a destination byte, and to give a transmit signal. The station watches for an empty slot; when one arrives it is marked full and the source, destination, and data fields filled in. The minipacket passes on its way, and eventually returns to the sending station. On the way it should have passed the destination, at which one of a variety possibilities will have occurred.

<u>No action</u> - the receiving station was switched off (or non-existent),

<u>Accepted</u> - the data and source bytes have been copied into the receiving station,

<u>Busy</u> - the receiving station was switched on but its reception register was not empty,

Unselected - the selection register in the receiving station had been set to exclude reception from this source.

The status is marked in the minipacket and reported to the originating station. The action to be taken by the sending host in the event that the minipacket was not accepted is not part of the definition of the Ring: different hosts may take different actions. The Ring does have a feature to prevent excess false traffic caused by a host looping sending minipackets that are not accepted. The more attempts are made to send the same minipacket the longer the report of its fate (unless accepted) is delayed in the station. Ultimately the bad news will be held up for sixteen Ring revolutions. When the minipacket returns to the sending station its content is compared bit by bit with what was sent, and the station interface includes a facility for reporting error. When a minipacket returns to the sending station it is always marked as empty and passed on. This is an anti-hogging device, and ensures that the bandwidth is shared out equally between the stations. It is not something that is visible to the system programmer at all.

One station is special and is called the **monitor station**. It is not connected to any host and its task is to set up and maintain the Ring framing, and to deal with the effects of obscure errors such as a slot being erroneously marked full. In order that the Ring may be readily maintainable, a variety of continuous checks are carried out by the monitor station and all other stations. This is done to detect faulty equipment early; a slightly defective repeater altering say one bit in 10^9 would otherwise pass unnoticed for a long time[2]. This continuous testing is a unique feature of the Cambridge Ring, but has little direct impact at the system level. The details of the fault detection mechanisms are not relevant here; it is sufficient to state that detected errors result in the transmission

---

[2] To avoid giving a false impression, it should be said that the interval between changes of repeater on practical Rings is measured in months or years, not days or weeks.

of a **maintenance minipacket** addressed to station zero. The use made of these is described in Section 6.4.

Between the station and the host come the **access circuits** which serve as interfaces between the station and a particular host. A great variety of access circuits exist, of widely varying degrees of sophistication. The crudest access circuits generate an interrupt whenever a minipacket arrives or has been successfully sent. This takes very little hardware, but leads to rather low throughput because most machines have difficulty keeping up with the high interrupt rate. A rapid sender sending continuous material to such a station will be likely to experience a considerable number of 'busies' and will have to retry repeatedly. Equally, a host transmitting by means of such an access circuit will not make anything like the best use of the Ring. To obtain ideal performance it is necessary to make a transmission request to the station within about 3.5 microseconds of the return of the previously transmitted minipacket[3]. Few machines if any can process a program interrupt that fast. Provided, however, that the machine in question does not habitually receive or send large amounts of data, the economy of circuits resulting from a program interrupt driven interface can be very worthwhile. In some cases the interface is similarly simple but interrupts the host's microcode. This typically means that the Ring will be serviced no later than the end of the instruction being executed when the interrupt was raised, so there is a good chance of meeting the timing requirements for optimum transmission. If the next level of protocol which involves blocks of information, logical channel numbers and checksums (the **packet protocol** - see

----

[3] The timing requirements for reception in ordinary circumstances are much less stringent since minipackets from a particular sender will be separated by at least the time required for a minipacket to circulate around the Ring.

below) is implemented in microcode, very good performance is possible.

More elaborate interfaces move the material to and from the host by DMA. In this case it is possible (though not necessary) to make additional performance gains by arranging that the packet protocol is handled in the interface. This relieves the host of substantial overheads such as checksum calculation as will be seen later. Such interfaces are typically based on fast microcomputers that on one side simply poll the signals from a station and drive DMA circuits on the other.

Finally, as a sort of special case, there are simple microcomputers that just poll the station signals. They are only able to receive or transmit when in a loop; the station signals are mapped into the machine's address space and must be polled at regular intervals in order to meet the various timing constraints. This approach is taken when machines are provided for simple services which do not require transfer of large amounts of data in haste. They may be thought of as hosts with integral access circuits.

It is characteristic of the Cambridge Ring that the unit of data that has to be received synchronously is very small, just two bytes. Because of this, high or low performance interfaces can be made available optionally as practical needs and finance dictate. In general, extra high performance requires more elaborate and expensive access circuits.

There are some applications for which direct use of minipackets is appropriate, because the information to be transmitted consists of disjoint small pieces of material at a low total data rate. Point-to-point digital telephony is an example, and the Ring has been successfully used in this way. Pairs of samples from an ordinary 64 kHz speech digitiser are sent in single minipackets at the rate of one pair every 256 microseconds. Usually, however, it is desirable to aggregate minipackets into larger units, and a description of the standard way to do this follows.

3.3 The packet protocol

Almost all communication round the Ring takes the form of **packets**[4] consisting of up to 1024 data minipackets, that is 2048 bytes of data. The format is simply defined as follows:

- One header minipacket
- One route minipacket
- Up to 1024 data minipackets
- One checksum minipacket

The header minipacket has ten bits defining the number of data minipackets, a fixed pattern to facilitate recognition, and a two bit field which gives type information to be defined later. The route minipacket has a twelve bit field known as the port number to give a logical channel into the host, together with four bits which may be used to characterise, at a higher level, the type of the packet. The checksum minipacket is a 16 bit sum of all minipackets including header and port, computed modulo $2^{16}-1$, i.e. with end-around carry.

Typical implementations of the packet protocol proceed as follows, considering reception first. The receiving station starts with its selection register open, so that minipackets from any source will be accepted. Minipackets that do not conform to the format rules for headers are discarded. On receipt of a header minipacket, the selection register is set to accept minipackets from the source of the header only, and the route minipacket awaited. On its arrival, a check is made that a packet is in fact expected from the relevant source and with the defined port. In general, if the packet is expected the host will have a buffer pre-assigned specifically for it and the ensuing data minipackets will be read into the buffer. At the end the checksum is checked and the select

---

[4] Readers from a different culture may think of a packet as a datagram. It is also the unit of forwarding in a ring-ring bridge, a topic outside the scope of this book.

register set to accept from all senders. If the packet was satisfactorily received, higher levels of software are notified.

The packet definition says nothing about selection, and it would be open to a suitably hardy implementor to arrange to receive several in parallel. For this and other reasons nothing is said in the definition about what to do if the source and route do not correspond to anything expected. Some implementations swallow and then ignore the whole packet (which is what happens in the corresponding case for an Ethernet packet), whereas some set the select register to reject everything for a short period. The intent here is that there is no other reason for a data minipacket to receive an unselected response. It is a broad hint to the sender that his material is being rejected by the recipient and he might as well stop sending it.

The following is a typical implementation of sending a packet.

1 Send the header. If the response is busy try to send the header again. If the response is unselected the header of the packet may be tried again or an attempt may be made to send packets intended for other destinations before trying this header packet again.

2 Send the route. If the response is busy, try again, if unselected give up.

3 Send the data. If there is an unselected response, give up. Retry on busies.

4 Send the checksum under the same rules as the data.

It is legitimate to send several packets (to different physical destinations) in parallel. No current implementations do so.

Both sending and reception of packets require the use of time constants after which the action in question is abandoned. Reception timeouts apply to entire packets and are of the order of 500–1000 ms. On transmission, all implementations that are capable of doing so proceed by counting attempts rather than by overall transmission timeouts. Typical figures are five hundred attempts to send a header and fifty attempts to send subsequent minipackets; it should be recalled that inability to send a header may well be caused by the receiver having set its selection register to receive only from another station from which it is accepting a packet.

Two minor options in the packet protocol are mentioned for the sake of completeness. The type bits in the header minipacket indicate whether the block is of the standard variety described or whether it is:

a) a literal data packet, in which the ten bits that normally give the length are themselves data and there are no further minipackets, or

b) a packet with zero where the checksum would ordinarily be found. This option was provided because it was expected that some implementations on very feeble hosts would not be able to compute the checksum.

Neither of these stunted options for packets are used much in practice.

A simple protocol implemented above the packet protocol is the **single shot protocol**. A large number of the management functions of the distributed system are implemented using it. The protocol consists of a few conventions about simple request-reply packet exchanges. The conventions are sketched to give the flavour; data minipackets are referred to as 'datapkt'.

Request Packet

datapkt 0: a fixed pattern
datapkt 1: the port to be used for the reply
datapkt 2: a function number, zero if inapplicable
datapkt 3 and on:
parameters and data of request

Reply Packet

datapkt 0: a fixed pattern
datapkt 1: zero
datapkt 2: a return code, zero indicates success
datapkt 3 and on:
results and data of reply

A set of conventions has been adopted to regulate the assignment of return codes, so that some attempt may be made to interpret them without reference to extensive dictionaries. In particular, it is possible to write a general handler for the single shot protocol which will try again in most cases where it is reasonable to do so. This will be independent of the particular request being made, since the return codes for which retry is reasonable are independent of the purpose of a particular single shot protocol transaction. For the assistance of programs which have to provide textual error messages for users, a small service on the Ring produces textual messages as translations for return codes. The single shot protocol is generally used in the manner of a remote procedure call.

The packet protocol does not of itself constitute a reliable method for sending streams of data which will be acted upon before completion. There are no guarantees of delivery, and there is no acknowledgement of the reception of a packet as a packet; the only acknowledgement is of a higher level nature such as a single shot protocol reply.

For some applications, such as terminal handling and file transfer between machines with local discs where the high performance File Server protocols would be inappropriate[5], flow control is required to regulate the exchange of data. This requirement is met by the **byte stream protocol.** Flow control is achieved by the inclusion of request and acknowledgement commands in the packets of data exchanged by the communicating parties. Byte streams are bi-directional so commands

---

[5] See Section 4.2 for more details about the File Server protocols.

and data in one direction are interleaved with the acknowledgements in the reverse direction. One problem that can arise, even with an orderly exchange of packets, is that one party may send the next packet in sequence before the other has completed internal processing of the previous packet. Given the rules of the packet protocol, this could lead to the apparent loss of such a packet. By a symmetrical argument, it is possible that an acknowledgement packet could be lost resulting in the retransmission of data, thereby duplicating data. Accordingly byte stream protocol packets contain a sequence number, and all request and acknowledgement commands indicate where in the sequence they apply. In this way lost or repeated data will be detected so that the correct ordering of bytes carried across the stream will be maintained. As a side effect, if a packet is lost because of the unlikely event of minipacket corruption on the Ring, retransmission will occur automatically and the byte stream will be error free. A full specification of the protocol, including details about the way in which byte streams are opened and closed, is given in the Appendix together with some remarks about implementation issues.

It is customary to relate, or to attempt to relate, the structure of any communication system and the protocols for its use to the ISO Model of Architecture for Open Systems Interconnection. The layers for which the model is so well-known are present because they represent, to the devisers of the model, levels at which there may be significant choices for implementation. In a system based around a single local network, the assignment of functions to layers becomes somewhat arbitrary. In the present case it is clear what constitutes the physical layer: the wires and optical fibres, modulation methods, repeaters and so on. The data-link layer includes stations, addressing and minipackets. The packet protocol is a network layer notion, though the reasons for this assertion are not evident from anything discussed in this chapter or book. If two rings are bridged together, then the packet is the unit of transfer across the bridge and nothing below the packet is transferable. On a single ring, minipacket transactions may be used if desired. The single-shot and the byte stream protocols are clearly transport-level notions.

3.4 Ring performance

The Ring, as already stated, has a raw data rate of 10 megabits/second. If we assume that the gap is short, the system transmission rate for useful data will be 10*16/38 or just over four megabits/second. This will be shared between all hosts seeking to transmit; there is only one bulk transmission at a time in progress (often there will be none). The point-to-point data rate depends upon the number of slots in the Ring. A slot used for transmission is passed on empty after it returns to the sender. In the prototype implementation, the next minipacket cannot be used either. Thus, if there are n minipackets in the Ring, an individual sending host can only use 1/(n+2) of the total capacity, obtaining 4/(n+2) megabits per second of data transmission. Detailed analysis shows that if there are m stations seeking to transmit as fast as they can, each will get 1/(n+m) of the total bandwidth if m>2, but 1/(n+2) if m=1 or m=2[6].

A number of measurements have been made of ring traffic when the system as a whole is in normal use. A hundred samples each were taken over periods varying from one millisecond to one second. For each sample period we give in the table overleaf the highest observed utilisation, i.e. the maximum of the hundred samples, and also the mean.

Heavy loadings can be attained by suitably and carefully providing enthusiastic transmitters and willing receivers. In practice they do not arise, in part because of contention for a receiver. Although the Ring is not a contention system in the usual sense,

----

[6] It is necessary to re-emphasise here that the analysis refers to the specific type of Ring used for the developments reported in this book, and not to later versions.

Sample period	Maximum	Mean
1 ms	14%	3.7%
10 ms	19%	3.7%
100 ms	13%	3.4%
1 s	12%	3.1%

in use there is a certain amount of contention because implementations of the packet protocol, as described above, set the select register to receive from the packet source only. This means that header minipackets from other sources will be rejected, and the effect of this on transmitters is definitely one of perceived contention.

The Cambridge File Server

4.1 File servers

The purpose of file servers is to provide backing store for machines in a network and to make files readily accessible from other machines in the network. The precise function of a file server is open to debate. There is a spectrum of possible designs which reflect differing judgements as to those operations which should be supported by the file server itself and those which should be left to its clients.

At the extreme of simplicity, there is the remotely accessed real disc. The operations supported would be read page and write page, each operation having as one of its arguments a physical page address of the form <Cylinder Track Block>. Such a file server would work highly efficiently; its software would have very little to do at all. The designers of client programs, however, might be less happy with it for two different reasons. First, the allocation of space would be tedious; it would give rise to synchronisation problems unless the disc system were partitioned physically between clients. Secondly, there would be no convenient system for ensuring the integrity of the disc contents. As indicated, there would be no requirement that different clients recorded allocations made in the same way: they might have quite different directory structures and naming conventions. The possible extent of client-independent clean-up and recovery would be almost nil, with a consequent replication of code in the clients for this purpose. It seems desirable to have some higher level of organisation known to the file server.

Next comes a system that may simply be described as a virtual disc. Such a system at its crudest would have as primitive operations allocate page, free page, read page and write page. In such a system the response to an allocate page request would probably be a unique page identifier, and this would be used in read page and write page requests. The identifier would probably not be a physical address, for the following reason. It is expedient to be able to check whether the address given in a read page or write page request is legitimate, that is to say whether the page referred to is in fact allocated. This could be done by marking the content of the page or by having a separate data structure accessed on a lookaside basis. For example, in parallel with the seek phase of a read page request, the file server could refer to a simple bitmap to check that the page was allocated. In practice a different sort of address would probably be chosen which allowed for more flexibility and some security. If the given identifier is turned into a physical address by a suitable translation procedure, flexibility is gained because the binding between the client's identifier and the physical material is under the server's control. There is also the advantage of being able to isolate bad tracks or pages easily. If the identifier is chosen from a space that is very sparsely occupied, there is a measure of protection against accidental use of incorrect identifiers. These two possibilities are more or less independent, in the sense that features of one may be combined with those of the other. For example, it is possible to issue identifiers which combine the physical address with a large field chosen essentially at random. In this case it is not possible to vary the binding between identifiers and physical disc pages very easily, but there is the advantage of sparseness as a guard against error.

If the points just mentioned are taken seriously, a particular kind of virtual disc system may be considered as being based on the ideas of capabilities. Capabilities are usually thought of, in hardware implementations, as unforgeable tickets of permission to perform some operation, and, when applied in the design of processors, as being protected by segregation into special segments or by tagging in the machine's memory. The unforgeability is gained by forbidding ordinary instructions to alter the content of capability segments in the one case, or by making ordinary data instructions destroy a capability tag in the other. Capabilities may be passed between procedures or processes, and this is done to give a computation activated by call or message the authority to carry out the actions called for. If it is arranged that in a virtual disc file server the identifiers are drawn from such a sparsely occupied space, the chance of any person or program guessing or computing a valid identifier may be regarded as zero. The identifiers themselves may then be treated as capabilities and no further access restriction need be imposed[1].

A capability-based virtual disc system is a considerable advance over a simple remote disc service, but still leaves a great deal of work to its clients. This may be seen by considering how very little such a server can do to assist the client. It can check that the set of blocks for which capabilities exist and the set of free blocks are exclusive and exhaustive - and that is all. Any organisation of blocks into higher level constructs is the responsibility of the client, and no help is available to him in doing it. It is not desirable, however, that all responsibility should be removed from the client, as the next example shows.

At the other end of the spectrum there lies what may be called the file repository. This term is used to refer to an arrangement in which the file server

---

[1] The analogy between sparse identifiers and capabilities in hardware is not complete. In particular, it is possible to assume in a capability-based computer that a capability is what it appears to be, and often also to determine for what type of object it is a capability, without using it. Capabilities whose unforgeability comes from sparseness need to be exercised to be validated, since the only way to distinguish them from arbitrary bit patterns is to present them for use.

handles almost all of the organisation of material for the client. A repository is rather like a multiple-access system in which only the commands appropriate to files exist. The user may log in to the repository, authenticate himself, and then make requests for various actions. For example, the contents of a directory may be examined and updated, directories may be created, and files may be moved to or copied from the repository. The repository deals with access controls and maintains the integrity of the directory structure. Like any other filing system, it has an essentially fixed set of naming conventions. Such a system has many advantages. It provides a useful service with a minimum of client code, and it can maintain a good level of integrity because of the amount of structure available to it. It certainly supports the notion of a file which the virtual disc server did not: it knows which collections of blocks or pages constitute files or directories. It can check accordingly that the files referred to in directory entries are complete and of the size stated, that they are disjoint, and that their internal structures are well-formed. It can check that disc space not referred to in directories is all marked as free. In short it can do as much consistency checking as could reasonably be required. This has however been achieved at the cost of fixing the naming structure and directory organisation, an action which has removed the flexibility of the server designs mentioned above.

The Cambridge File Server occupies an intermediate design position between a virtual disc server and a repository. It is an implementation of what Birrell and Needham called a **Universal File Server**[2]. In this design the intention was to augment a virtual disc service by a naming substrate which would provide the desired coherence without committing the clients to any specific conventions at the level of text names or directory structure. Indeed, it was a design

---

[2] A.D. Birrell & R.M. Needham. September 1980. 'A Universal File Server'. IEEE Transactions on Software Engineering, New York, SE-6(5), 450-453.

requirement that the server should be able to support several name or directory structures at the same time. Since the local implementation which will be described below has most of the attributes of the general design it will be unnecessary to go into detail here, but some points of principle will be mentioned. A Universal File Server supports two classes of objects, called **files** and **indices**. A file is an uninterpreted vector of bytes, and has a unique identifier that is permanent and never re-used. This identifier is also chosen from a sufficiently sparse space that it may be assumed unforgeable and considered as a capability in the sense described previously. Operations on files are performed on the basis of the identifier, hereinafter referred to as a **PUID** (Permanent Unique Identifier). The commitment the server makes is to maintain a file in existence as long as its PUID is recorded in an index that is accessible from a fixed **root index**. Indices also have PUIDs, and the PUID of an index may be recorded in another index (or in itself) just like the PUID of a file. The structure of indices thus constitutes a general naming network. PUIDs may be stored in more than one index and looped structures are possible. Accordingly it is not sufficient in general to rely on reference counts to reveal that an object ought to be discarded and general garbage collection facilities have to be provided. It may be noted that the garbage collection task is not enormous, since the name-containers that have to be scanned consist only of the indices which will in all practical circumstances be far less numerous than files.

It is up to client systems to make use of the index facility as they will. One client system might have a complex structure of directories and also an index corresponding to each directory, whereas another might have a single index in which all PUIDs from a filing system were recorded. In the latter case, the structure of the filing system would not be mirrored at all by an index structure. It should be noted that indices are entirely separate from directories, and for a very good reason. Indices are objects known to the file server implementation, as they have to be for the commitment on file existence to be discharged. The format of an index is thus fixed by the design of the server, whereas the designers of individual client systems ought to be free to design directories to suit their own requirements. The information directories contain is variable depending on textual naming conventions, access controls, accounting methods, and so on.

Various attributes may be associated with files in a server of the type being discussed. Some are there for purposes internal to the server: examples are the size and a default pattern to be used when part of a file is read without previously having been written. Others are not interpreted by the server at all, but are kept with the file for external convenience: notes as to the file structure would be examples. The server can make no guarantee of the accuracy of any attributions of the second type.

Another area of design choice, to a considerable extent independent of the choices just outlined, concerns questions of interlock and atomicity. To what extent should the file server provide facilities for exclusive access to material and for causing compound actions to appear atomic? It has been usual to place the responsibility for interlocking on the server itself, but there is another choice. In the universal design it is expected that naming and access control management will be done outside the server (quite possibly using data stored within the server); exclusive access and locking can, in principle, be handled outside too. Suppose that a certain set S of files is under the control of a management system M, where M may reside on a single machine or on several. A practical requirement for this is to arrange that capabilities for the files in the set are never passed outside M's control, because if they were allowed to escape then M would no longer be able to take responsibility for the treatment of the files themselves. A consequence of this is that all access to a file in S must be handled by M, since otherwise the capability for the file could not be available and the file would be inaccessible. Accordingly, it is possible for M to provide whatever constraints on access to files that it is desired to implement. All that it is necessary to provide in the server is whatever set of facilities is deemed necessary for mediating the sharing of files which are not under a common management in the sense outlined. These can be much less complex than would be needed to meet more general requirements.

On the subject of integrity there is relatively little to be said. The integrity requirements of file servers do not differ greatly from those of more conventional filing systems and may be met by similar techniques.

4.2 The Cambridge File Server

This section describes in detail the File Server implemented as part of the Cambridge Distributed Computing System.

The external interface is described first. All reference to files from outside is in terms of capabilities, which are 64-bit quantities. The client is expected to assume that capabilities cannot be guessed and accordingly to rely on a file being inaccessible to anyone who has not been given the capability from an authorised possessor of it. The capabilities are not in fact completely unstructured, as will be seen later in the section on implementation. Capabilities may be stored anywhere, not excluding outside the system altogether, for example by being written on a piece of paper. External storage, however, is not sufficient to guarantee that the file will remain in existence, and special steps must be taken to ensure this.

A file is a sequence of sixteen-bit words, starting at offset 0 and finishing at offset size-1, where the size was declared when the file was created or altered subsequently by suitable commands to the server. Commands for reading and writing files may act on any contiguous sequence of words, as for example 19 to 36, or 0 to 94304. When a file is created one of the arguments is the pattern that should be delivered by the server if a previously unwritten word of the file is read. Such a read operation is not an error: it is quite proper to think of the create operation as bringing into existence a file of the specified number of words all containing the given initial pattern. Indeed, this is how the client should think of it.

All transactions with the File Server take place using simple and (as far as possible) repeatable protocols based on the single shot protocol described in Section 3.3. Wherever the transmission of commands or data are mentioned, this should be understood as taking place by the despatch of packets or sequences of packets without any flow control, a point considered further below. The sequentiality of the Ring prevents any disorder problems. The File Server listens to commands on a port number which is delivered to clients by the Name Server. Each request carries with it at least one reply port. In many cases there is only one, as in requests to give the size of a file; however, in the particular case of the read command there are two, so that the data may be sent on one and a status report on the other. A request may also be given a tag, which is simply an identifier assigned by the client and the File Server will append the tag to the reply. The tag is used completely at the discretion of the client. Its main utility is to distinguish replies to different requests in the case that the client does not see fit to use different port numbers for them. One case where this may happen is that of retry after a request was apparently lost and timed out.

Administrative commands such as READ FILE SIZE and CHANGE FILE SIZE are conventional examples of the single shot protocol. The only point worthy of remark is that the latter command must be specified as changing _to_ a value rather than _by_ a value, to secure repeatability. The READ command is slightly more elaborate. It specifies the file identifier, first word, and last word, together with a port to which the material should be returned. The File Server will then send the requested material as a series of unlabelled packets which contain nothing but data. Since the user may request reading beyond the end of the file, or from a non-existent file, or may do something else calling for comment, the request is required to specify another port to which a response will be sent after data despatch is complete. The WRITE command is very similar, with one more stage of interchange. The File Server replies to the original request with a "Go Ahead" packet, nominating the File Server port to which the data is to be sent and indicating readiness to receive an unvarnished string of packets with no flow control. Again a status report goes to the client at the end of the transfer.

Simplified read and write commands called SSPREAD and SSPWRITE are provided to deal with the case where only small bodies of up to 256 words of data are involved. SSPREAD includes the data with the status report, and SSPWRITE appends it to the command packet. The provision of these commands recognises that there is a tradeoff to be made between the overhead of packet send and receive on the one hand and costs of separating data from protocol material on the other.

It should be reiterated that there is no flow control provided on reading or demanded on writing. Accordingly, it is the responsibility of a client machine not to call for more material than can be accommodated in memory available to it as everything he asks for will be sent regardless. Equally it is up to the implementor to be able to accept the material offered when writing as fast as the user can send it. This is the more severe constraint in practice. Equally, there is no retransmission of individual packets in case of erroneous transmission. Failure of one of the packets read will cause the whole to be asked for again; loss of a packet read will cause timeout at the recipient and eventual total retransmission. This, and the corresponding arrangements for writing, illustrate the exploitation of the reliability characteristic of modern local communications in general and the Ring in particular.

One of the few compromises it was necessary to make in the interest of efficient implementation is the distinction between _normal_ and _special_ files. The distinction is made when a file is created and its status cannot subsequently be changed. A write command is guaranteed to change a special file atomically whereas there is no guarantee about writing to a normal file. The difference is of importance in the case of failure of the server, the client, or the Ring. It is up to the client to create files of suitable mode. For example, the CAP system uses special files for its directories but files made on behalf of users are normal. To implement all files as special would give a tidier interface to the user but would indubitably have some performance implications.

As outlined in the discussion above of universal file servers, there is also a system of indices with the rule that a file is only guaranteed to remain in existence if its identifier is recorded in an index. Indices are simply special files with an additional distinguishing mark. Whenever a file is created, the client must nominate an index and offset for the PUID of the new file to be recorded in. The new PUID is not returned to the caller until the change to the index is committed. This is an operation that has to be carefully defined and implemented in order to be repeatable in some reasonable sense. Suppose that a reply is lost. Simple repetition by the caller will cause another PUID to be created and deposited in the same index at the same place. The old one will be lost. A really cautious client will repeat his request with a different tag or reply port to deal with long delay problems.

The commands relating to indices will now be sketched. They are all single shot protocol commands of an obvious sort. CREATE FILE and CREATE INDEX are given the size of the thing to be created and also the PUID and offset of an index slot in which the created object's PUID may be preserved. This is not optional, and the entire command will fail if the index slot is inaccessible for any reason. These commands return the created PUID. RETRIEVE requires an index PUID and offset and returns the content. The PUID found in the index is not checked in any way. In the RETAIN command the PUID offered for preservation is checked for validity and the object's reference count increased. In due course the reference count of any PUID overwritten in the index will be decremented, though this need not be done before replying to the caller. READ INDEX SIZE and CHANGE INDEX SIZE are obvious. Changing the size of an index downwards causes reference counts to be decremented for any PUIDs preserved in the discarded part of the index.

One of the indices is distinguished as the **root index.** It is important in relation to continued retention of files and indices, since the File Server guarantees that a file will remain in being for at least as long as a PUID for the file exists in an index accessible from the root index. The root index is also of importance since possessing a capability for it makes access to all files possible; it is of some importance to treat this particular bit pattern as a secret. It may be noted that client subsystems do not need to have the root index capability: for example, the TRIPOS operating system has a capability for the index which is at the root of the TRIPOS filing system, not for the root index of the File Server.

It was explained above how exclusive access facilities need only be provided by the File Server to a limited extent. The server supports exclusive access to single files by means of the OPEN and CLOSE commands. An OPEN command is either rejected or returns a temporary capability known as a **TUID** for the file in question. Until CLOSE or timeout the file may only be accessed using the TUID, so that provided the recipient keeps it to itself or only distributes it in a suitable manner, the desired synchronisation effects will follow. The locking mechanism takes account of the distinction between normal files and special files. If a special file is opened, all operations upon it until the close are collectively atomic, so that either they all happen or none of them do. The CLOSE operation itself commits or abandons the series of operations. Since it may be desired to commit or abandon a series of operations without relinquishing exclusive access, an additional ENSURE command is provided to do just that. ENSURE when applied to normal files is not very useful. There is a timeout of fifteen minutes associated with a TUID. It is reset whenever the TUID is used. If the timeout expires, the File Server will break the interlock on the corresponding file.

The interfaces just described have some slightly unobvious consequences. Unlike a capability system in a single machine, there is no control over where capabilities have been stored. Accordingly it is possible for a client to present a capability for preservation in an index before, during, or after a decision that the object referred to by the capability is inaccessible from the root index. It may be that the object has already been discarded, in which case the attempt to retain the capability must fail, or it may be that the decision is in progress in which case it may be abandoned. What is essential is that successful preservation of a capability must maintain in existence the whole of a structure which the preservation makes accessible rather than just parts of it. The important case is where the capability being preserved is a capability for an index which itself contains many capabilities for other files and indices. It is naturally desirable to be able to deal with the consequences of production of a capability from the outside up to the last possible moment, but the consistency requirement is overriding. A natural further consequence is that before a capability is preserved it must be checked for validity.

Another implication of what has been said is that the File Server is able to get into a state where there are detached looped structures inaccessible from the root index, and genuine garbage collection is needed. The implementation of such a garbage collector for the Cambridge File Server will be described later.

4.3 Implementation issues

A major decision in file server design concerns the representation of objects. The requirements are to be able to implement the external operations on objects in as effective a way as possible and to make the best use of disc space. When balancing these sometimes conflicting demands, it is also necessary to take into account the ease, or otherwise, of implementing whatever atomic update properties are required. The Cambridge File Server represents its objects (files and indices) in a variety of formats according to size while taking great care to make the differences of representation invisible at the interface to the client. The goal here was to make good use of space and also to minimise the number of disc accesses when making simple use of small objects.

In order to make the discussion clear, some detail about the disc layout is required. On each cylinder there are 21 small blocks of 512 bytes and 42 large blocks of 2048 bytes. This distribution was expected to make best use of the disc surfaces on the basis of studies of the content of existing file systems in the Computer Laboratory. The controller used is able to transfer more than one block in a single disc command according to a chain set up when the disc is formatted. This facility is used to arrange that a specific small block called the <u>cylinder map</u> may be read in the same command as any of the small blocks. Every object represented in the File Server has a header which is a small block. This contains information about the object type, size, initial pattern and so forth and also for rather small objects, containing no more than 244 words of data, the data part itself. If an operation upon an object requires the object to become larger than 244 words then the object is transparently reformatted as a medium object. Medium objects have their data held in large blocks, the disc addresses of which are recorded in the header block. The maximum size of a medium object is thus 122 large blocks. Similarly, the representation may be changed from medium to large; a large object has two levels of map, the entries in its header block pointing to further small blocks themselves containing addresses of data blocks.

The size of an object as recorded in its header has little to do with the actual space allocated to it. The size indicates an address such that attempts to write beyond it will not be successful. Physical disc blocks are allocated when the physical operation of writing takes place and requests to read from unwritten blocks return the initial pattern specified when the file was created, no disc transfers being involved. All objects are initially created small, i.e. with small representations, even if their declared size is immense. The format change, mentioned as occurring when a command requires it, is irreversible. No attempt is made to turn an object back into a small object just because there are less than 244 words of good data in it. This is for three reasons: first it is only possible to recognise the occasion for a downward reformat in particular circumstances; secondly it produces severe practical problems about atomicity; and thirdly, it is not needed much.

The unique identifier of a file contains as part of the bit-pattern the address of the header block, so that, given an identifier, the File Server can go straight to the header without any further lookup. This course is justified in the interest of efficiency provided that some escape is possible if the header block in question is damaged or becomes unusable for some other reason.

For each cylinder of the disc there is a cylinder map, at a fixed address in the cylinder, containing a description of the state and contents of each block on the cylinder. In the case of a header block, it records the fact that it is a header and includes the remaining 32 bits of unique identifier, originally generated at random when the object was created. Notice that, since the map is of necessity on the same cylinder as the header, the map may be chained as an automatic follow-on address for the disc controller. Care has been taken to dispose the small blocks in relation to the rotational position of the cylinder map in such a way that it is inexpensive to read the map (in order to check the bona fides of a presented identifier) after reading the header block. An alleged file identifier may be rejected out of hand if the address part does not indicate a small block. In the unlikely event of an allocated header block becoming corrupt and unwriteable, there is space in the cylinder map for the necessary indirection. Our approach here contrasts with that, for example, of a system developed at Xerox PARC in which all identifiers are looked up in a B-Tree[3]. However efficient that lookup may be made, it seemed to us to be worth while to omit stages of lookup wherever possible. The cylinder map also records, for all allocated blocks other than header blocks, the identity of the object to which they belong (in terms of header address) and the identity of the block in the object - data block m or intermediate map block n. This information provides the redundant backup for the contents of the header and map blocks and enables them to be reconstructed if need be. It does this without interfering with the data content of the large blocks, each of which contains 1024 words of unencumbered user data. Provision of the redundancy separately has the advantage that the maps may be checked for consistency by a recovery program scanning the disc after an error or malfunction has damaged the data structures on it, without having to read every single block.

The cylinder maps record the state of block allocations in a way designed to facilitate various kinds of transactional atomicity. A block may be in one of four states: deallocated, deallocated intended to be allocated, allocated, allocated intended to be deallocated. The intending states are transient, intentions being confirmed or denied according to a commit or decommit decision on a larger transaction. As explained earlier, the File Server supports atomic transactions on individual files, and accordingly the state of a transaction may be recorded in the cylinder map entry for the header of the file. The act of marking the map entry of a header as committed, for example, commits the completion of all allocation intentions marked on blocks of that file. The operation may easily be completed by the restart

---

[3] An excellent comparison and contrast of the Cambridge File Server with that system is given in J.G. Mitchell & J. Dion. April 1982. 'A Comparison of Two Network-Based File Servers'. _Communications of the Association for Computing Machinery, New York,_ 25(4), 233-245.

program which scans all the cylinder maps in the ordinary course. It takes no action on an observed intention until the header block entry is reached, after which the appropriate actions may be taken. On this basis, all requirements for atomic operations supported by the File Server are readily met if they are converted into allocation intentions by more or less conventional means.

The mechanism is used in this way to implement operations on special files, which, it will be recalled, are all atomic either within one File Server command or in an OPEN-CLOSE interval if these commands are used. Whenever a write is required to a particular block of such a file, the original block is marked 'allocated intended to be deallocated', a replacement block is found, marked 'deallocated intended to be allocated', and written to. If less than the whole of the block is to be written, the rest is properly initialised. Commitment or otherwise of the transaction as a whole is thus converted into commitment or otherwise of allocation intentions. It should be noted that the method adopted for dealing with special files does not preserve the layout of the file: commitment moves the data in effect to new blocks. This approach was taken because the incidence of files with a requirement for contiguity is low, and the present method avoids copying. It would not be hard to implement the other strategy.

Underlying these operations is the physical allocation and deletion of space. Allocation is done in a quite simple way; a free block of the required size is allocated on the cylinder nearest to a quoted 'home' block that contains suitable free space. The home for a header block is the index block in which the identifier was initially recorded at file creation; for an ordinary block of a file it is the preceding block (or the header if there is none). The allocation thus secured is in general terms satisfactory. There is probably not much gained by trying to keep a header block close to its initial index entry, but nothing is lost either.

One of the parameters recorded in the header block of a file is a reference count, indicating the number of indices in which the PUID of the file is recorded. No special care is taken to ensure the accuracy of this count; it is trivial to arrange that it has at least the proper value. This being so, an object may safely be deleted if its reference count is observed to be zero, and this is done. Since this is only intended to reduce the amount of work that has to be done by the garbage collector, it is again unnecessary to be particularly reliable. The rule adopted is simple and safe - if in doubt leave it to the garbage collector. In practice, the great majority of deletion occurs via this optimised route. The kind of genuine garbage that cannot be found on the basis of reference counts is not common; it mostly derives from the occurrence of radical changes to the structure of one of the client file management systems.

4.4 Garbage collection

In the Cambridge System, garbage collection of the File Server is carried out by a program running in a different machine allocated for the purpose as and when it is required. There are a variety of reasons for this (in addition to the obvious one that in an establishment working on distributed computing it seems wholly natural). First, it avoids interference with normal service as far as possible, and secondly it makes it easier to accomodate the rather extensive tables that build up in the course of garbage collection. The initiative for starting a garbage collection lies with the File Server program.

The garbage collection method is basically a familiar type of asynchronous algorithm. It is made simpler by two considerations. First, provided that the operation of committing the decision to delete garbage is properly atomic, the action taken in the event of failures of machines or unexpected occurrences can simply be to stop the garbage collection and start again. This occurs even if it would in principle be possible to recover by sufficiently complex code. Secondly, the requirement on a garbage collector is to find and delete material that is garbage and never to delete material that is not garbage: if in doubt, don't collect it. There is no requirement that the garbage collected should correspond to any instantaneous view of the system. On the other hand, it is made more complicated by the possibility that PUIDs may be remembered outside the system. If a client produces a PUID for preservation in an index, that preservation may make some elaborate structure of indices and files, previously inaccessible from the root and thus candidate garbage, into an accessible structure. That structure must either survive garbage collection completely or not at all; in the latter case the attempt to preserve the PUID must fail.

The procedure itself is now outlined. The File Server has a flag indicating whether or not the garbage collector is running. This is set as a result of the initial message from the garbage collector to the File Server and reset at the conclusion of collection. While the flag is on, the File Server reports by message to the garbage collector whenever a PUID is preserved in an index (the communication details are given later). This is interpreted by the garbage collector as indicating that the object belonging to the PUID is definitely not garbage - a conservative assumption since the index in which the PUID is being preserved might itself be garbage. Setting the flag also enables an interface by which the garbage collector can read all the cylinder maps and thus establish a table giving the PUIDs of all objects in existence and whether they are files or indices. The garbage collector program is equipped with the PUID of the root index and can carry out a conventional accessibility scan. The scan terminates when no accessible indices remain to be scanned and there are no outstanding preservation messages.

At this point the garbage collector has a list of candidate garbage, and can enter its next phase. This consists of making calls upon the File Server to mark the candidate garbage objects as <u>inhibited</u>. For the present, this has no effect on the way the File Server reacts to clients' commands relating to the objects; such commands of course must be making use of PUIDs stored outside the system, since there is necessarily no reference to such objects inside the accessible index structure. During this phase preservation messages may still arrive at the garbage collector, and these, are processed as in the previous phase (which is in fact called as a subroutine). It may happen that the result of such an action is to discover that an object is not garbage after it has been marked as inhibited; in this case the File Server must be called to remove the inhibition. Note that it is very important that this action be correctly carried out. In the absence of positive response from the File Server the entire operation is abandoned. This contrasts with the situation while setting inhibitions - failure there merely leads to a little inefficiency.

At the end of the 'set inhibits' phase, the entire operation may be committed subject to the crucial interlock that all preservation messages sent by the File Server have arrived at and been processed by the garbage collector. If this is not the case, processing has to continue until the condition is satisfied or the collection abandoned. Usually there will be no problem, and the File Server sets its <u>believe inhibits</u> flag. Once this flag has been set, the File Server refuses to accept any client commands relating to inhibited objects - they are regarded as non-existent. The garbage collector at its leisure goes through the garbage issuing commands to the File Server to destroy the unwanted material. The File Server restart program, used after a File Server failure, removes all inhibitions; if believe inhibits has been set it will delete the objects too.

It will be clear that the garbage collector has to be able to perform some very serious operations on the File Server, and there is an important authentication issue. The solution adopted is as follows. As previously stated, the initiative for running the garbage collector comes from the File Server itself. The File Server engages in a standard single shot protocol transaction with the Resource Manager, asking for a suitable machine to be allocated and giving the PUID of the file to be loaded into it. The PUID is that of a file containing the memory image of the garbage collector. Part of the Resource Manager's standard reply is the address of the machine allocated, and the File Server will then accept garbage collection requests from the machine mentioned and from nowhere else. Essentially, the integrity of the Resource Manager is relied on. It would be possible to go further - the File Server could put a one-time identifier in the image sent and require to receive it back on the first call. This would be more secure at the cost of making it necessary to fix the address in the image into which the one-time identifier is to be put.

It is evidently necessary that the communication of preservation messages should be secure, since missing one may cause something to be regarded as garbage when it is not. It is equally desirable that sending them should be an inexpensive operation, since it has to be done in the course of the relevant File Server command. The procedure adopted is as follows. The message itself is brief, consisting only of a PUID. The messages are serially numbered, and a circular buffer of about twenty of them is maintained in the File Server. At each preservation the buffer is updated and then sent in its entirety. This is very inexpensive since, as is usual in communication systems, short messages are dominated by software overheads. No response is awaited or given. On receipt of such a message the garbage collector checks the serial numbers and fills in any gap that may arise because of lost messages. Trouble only occurs if twenty such messages are lost in a row. This is unlikely, since they occur far enough apart in time (about every 1.5 seconds) to be regarded as independent with respect to transient Ring incidents. Even if twenty are lost in a row, there is a completely safe solution, namely to abandon the garbage collection, and this is done. At the end of the scanning phases of the garbage collection it is necessary to synchronise with the File Server. The message requesting that the believe inhibits flag be set is accompanied by the serial number of the last preservation message received by the collector. It is only acted upon if this is the same as that recorded in the File Server as associated with the last PUID preserved. This final interaction is the only communication from the garbage collector in relation to preservation messages, and occurs independently of any commands given to the File Server by its clients.

4.5 Typical users

In practice at Cambridge, the root index contains a small number of entries which are themselves the roots of subsystems of various sorts. We shall outline three of these which have very different properties.

One set of files contain support material for the system of small servers. An example is the file used by the Name Server to back up its tables. The PUID of this file is bound into the Name Server's code and the file need not have a textual name in any filing system at all. The PUID is, of course, recorded in an index so that the file continues to exist, but the index does not correspond to any directory. These very low-level functions do not need any of the facilities of an ordinary filing system, and should not be required to use them since to do so would introduce undesirable dependency loops into the structure as a whole, making any change or development of the filing system very hazardous.

The TRIPOS operating system makes use of the File Server in a quite different way. The TRIPOS file system has a conventional hierarchy of directories, a file being recorded in one directory only so that the structure of directories and files is strictly a tree. The system is intended to be convenient and useful for a group of friendly people and there is no emphasis on protection at all. The representation chosen uses one File Server index and one special file to correspond to each TRIPOS directory. Therefore, creating a file with a certain title in a particular directory involves recording its PUID in the appropriate index as well as putting the appropriate entry in the directory which, to re-emphasise a point, is regarded by the File Server as a completely standard file. The PUID occupies the same place in a TRIPOS directory as a disc address would in a local-disc version of that system. TRIPOS is run on the processing servers, and the operating system as it is loaded into a machine allocated to run TRIPOS contains the file system code. TRIPOS may be running in several machines at the same time, so the filing system code makes use of File Server interlocks when necessary to regulate concurrent access from the various machines.

It would have been possible to have proceeded differently by having a single index associated with the entire TRIPOS filing system. Then it would have been necessary to record in a TRIPOS directory the offset in the master index at which the PUID was to be found, in order that the file could be deleted correctly. Space management in the master index would not have been very difficult, since there would never be more than one entry referring to a PUID. This course was rejected on efficiency grounds.

Finally the File Server is host to the CAP filing system. The CAP itself is described elsewhere[4]. It is a shared machine which now has the Ring as its only peripheral, though originally it had the usual complement of directly attached devices. Its filing system constitutes a general naming network, and is based on the preservation of capabilities in directories[5]. The CAP operating system is based on swapping segments, where a segment is the same as a file (sometimes a window onto a file); segments are swapped in place, to and from their permanent homes in the filing system. When the CAP operating system was modified to use the File Server instead of local disc, it became evident that the organisation provided by

---

[4] M.V. Wilkes & R.M. Needham. 1979. The Cambridge CAP Computer and its Operating System. New York: North Holland Publishing Company.

[5] And some other forms of protected name-container, but these details are not necessary here.

the File Server was sufficiently like that underlying the CAP operating system that the sensible course of action was to remove as much of the file management as possible from the operating system and make the best use of the File Server structure. Accordingly, an index was set up to correspond with each directory and many parts of the CAP operating system below the directory level were abolished. However, it was necessary to have some additional apparatus using the File Server for the following reason. The CAP operating system is capability-based, and the basic retrieve operation on a directory is to request and receive a capability for a named object. If the directory entry is subsequently deleted, the capability in the hands of the user remains valid. In the earlier implementation of the system the existence of a capability in the currently active virtual memory was readily noticed and the existence of an object could be controlled by a temporary reference count of capabilities in current use as well as a permanent reference count of capabilities preserved in directories[6]. In the new implementation it was not sufficient to remember inside CAP that capabilities were in active issue for an object, since the decision to abandon an object is taken in the File Server. Accordingly, there is an additional index called the Active Object Index in which the PUIDs of all objects with capabilities in current use are recorded. The ramifications of doing this without gross inefficiency were described by Dellar[7].

----

[6] CAP also had an asynchronous garbage collector for its file system.

[7] C.N.R. Dellar. October 1980. 'Removing Backing Store Administration from the CAP Operating System'. Operating Systems Review, New York, 14(4), 41-9.

Small Servers

5.1 Introduction

This chapter is concerned with the details of the small servers used to implement the great majority of services in the Cambridge Distributed System. In Chapter One how the idea of stand-alone machines providing static services has developed in distributed systems was explained. At Cambridge, the concept has been taken further whereby the distribution of services is along functional lines. Each server only provides a single service so that there shall be true independence between services. A consequence of this approach is the need for a plethora of simple, inexpensive machines to support fine-grained distribution. Furthermore, it becomes increasingly necessary as the number of servers grows that control over them should be largely automatic in order that starting the system from cold and recovery after errors can proceed without human involvement.

This chapter presents a description of the construction of small servers, their management, and the standard software packages for use by services. Individual services, in terms of their function and implementation, form the subject of the succeeding chapter.

5.2 Small server construction

Nearly twenty small servers have been built in the Computer Laboratory based on the Z80 microprocessor. The physical construction of the servers has been modified a number of times and the following description relates to the most recent versions. To the programmer, all versions of the servers are identical except for some variation in memory size.

A server is packaged as a single wire-wrapped card, measuring approximately 7.5 inches square, containing a Z80 processor, Ring access circuit, 1K bytes of read-only memory, 32K bytes of dynamic random access memory and associated decoding and refresh logic, adding up to a total of about forty chips. The Ring access circuit is extremely simple; the internal registers of a station are mapped onto memory addresses, outside the range of actual memory. Software in the Z80 has to handle minipackets directly and implement higher level protocols without any further hardware assistance. A library of subroutines for driving the Ring has been written in support of the standard protocols. There is little need for the small servers to have more powerful Ring access circuits, because generally they are used for applications that do not require high data rates or overlapped computation and data transfer. The read-only memory is used to hold standard code for bootstrapping and debugging the server, together with a collection of subroutines for driving the packet protocol.

A socket on the circuit card gives access to the major logic signals of the system so that an auxiliary card holding circuits to interface to a device or special purpose application hardware can be connected to the processor. The use of separate processor and application circuit cards allows for some flexibility during testing and repair because of the interchangeability of the units.

The simplicity of the servers enables them to be constructed cheaply; the raw component cost is about £100. This figure does not include power supplies, cabinets, repeaters or station units. Early models of the servers were packaged individually, mainly because they were intended to connect peripherals to the Ring and had to be located in close proximity to the devices concerned. The more recent versions can be collected together into groups sharing the same case and power supplies, thereby reducing the overall cost. A further lowering of cost comes from the development of a special attachment to a repeater, called a **repeater extender**, that enables up to six stations to be connected to the Ring from a single repeater. This device is well suited for connecting a box full of small servers to the Ring. When programming a new service, the additional cost of making a new small server is held to be comparable to the manpower costs of installing a new process into a shared machine and ensuring that it does not interfere with software already there. In addition, there are all of the advantages outlined in Chapter One that stem from the ability to develop software on a dedicated machine.

The physical limitations of the small servers have a pronounced influence on the way in which they are used. An important point is that the machines are too small to support a filing system or to run compilers for high level languages. Furthermore, the machines generally have no direct terminal connections. These factors led to the development of a system for remote control of the servers so that software development could take place on larger, more powerful computers. A programmer can therefore work on a small server, even though it is located some distance away from him. One important benefit that comes from using a larger machine for programming services is that it allows the use of high level languages and powerful program development aids.

5.3 SBOOT

The control program found in the read-only memory (ROM) of small servers is called **SBOOT** and an identical copy is placed in each server. Any service can be run by any machine, apart from those services tied to special devices. SBOOT implements a minimum set of primitives needed to enable the server to communicate across the Ring, to down-line load code and to provide support for remote debugging. There is a deliberate intention to keep SBOOT as simple as possible so that the likelihood that it contains errors is small and so that it will fit into the 1K bytes of ROM provided on these machines. All of the more complicated aspects of small server management are left to a special server called the **Boot Server.** Thus, for example, SBOOT takes no part in control over who can install a new version of a service, but relies instead upon protection within the Boot Server. Any changes in the way that small servers are controlled can be made by alteration of the Boot Server alone, without disturbing the copy of SBOOT in each of the servers.

5.4 Program loading

It is best for several reasons that the initiative to reload the program into a small server should come from the SBOOT control program. One is that it is possible to replace a faulty server _in situ_ and have the new machine reload the service without any further action being necessary. This is very useful if the system has to be restarted after a complete shutdown such as occurs with a major power failure and it also makes it possible for engineering personnel to replace suspect equipment with only a minor disruption to the system as a whole. In addition, the arrangements for dealing with software errors (which will be described in Section 5.5) ensure that a service is be reloaded if it crashes so that the small servers are tolerant of failure and will to a considerable degree recover automatically.

When a small server is powered on, or an external reset switch is depressed, the server will enter a program loading routine in SBOOT. This routine initially goes to the **Name Server** to look up the name of a loading service called 'BOOT'. This service is one of those provided by the Boot Server. SBOOT then sends off a single shot protocol request packet to the loading service. The reply packet from the Boot Server is followed by a train of packets containing the program to load into the server's random access memory (RAM). The reply packet contains the loading address for the data in the first packet of the train, and each packet contains the loading address for the next packet in sequence. The last packet contains a special marker to indicate that no further packets follow. SBOOT restarts the loading operation from the beginning if the Boot Server fails to send a well-formed chain of packets within a reasonable time. Normally this will only happen if a communication error causes one of the packets in the chain to be lost or rejected. Once the program is loaded, SBOOT transfers control to a standard location in the RAM so that the service program will start running.

When it receives a load request, the Boot Server has to determine which program to send to the server. Since the SBOOT program is service independent, it cannot yield this information. Instead the Boot Server sends the station number from which it has accepted a request to the Name Server _reverse name look up_ service. This service will translate the station number of the server into a mnemonic machine name. The Boot Server contains tables that relate machine names to the files holding the code for services and so can select the appropriate file on the basis of the answer from the Name Server.

It is desirable that it should be possible to reload small servers independently of the Boot Server on two grounds: the first is that it must be possible to run the system even if the Boot Server is not operational, perhaps because of a hardware fault, and the second is that, for testing new versions of services or running _ad hoc_ programs, it is inconvenient to have to install them in the Boot Server first. The requirement is met by arranging that if SBOOT fails to get a positive response from the Boot Server within twenty seconds of issuing a loading request, it allows a further twenty seconds to see if a single shot protocol request arrives, directed to a special loading port in itself, from any machine. If such a request does not arrive in time, SBOOT tries the Boot Server again and so on until eventually there is a response.

The request sent to the loading port contains a Ring address that SBOOT can contact in order to get a program to load using the normal protocol. The source of such a request usually comes from a program called 'Z80LOAD' which can be run on a number of machines. The parameters of the Z80LOAD program include the name of a machine to load and a file name for the program to be loaded. As an example, suppose that the machine called 'PRINTER' enters the program loading sequence and does not receive a reply from the Boot Server because the Boot Server is not running. If the Z80LOAD program is run with the name PRINTER supplied as its argument, the program will first of all look up the name 'LOAD-PRINTER' in the Name Server to determine the Ring address of the loading port for PRINTER. Then it sends off a request to PRINTER giving a route back to itself as the address for sending loading requests to. This causes the copy of SBOOT in the machine PRINTER to send such a request to the Z80LOAD program and get back program code in return. Once the server has been loaded, it forgets about the route to the Z80LOAD program and the next time the server reloads it will start off by trying the Boot Server as before.

If the Boot Server is approached by a small server for which it has no loading file, a default program is loaded which will wait for a loading request from any machine. In this case, code will be loaded into the server by use of the Z80LOAD program. This mode of operation is typically used when a service is under development and not ready for installation in the Boot Server as an operational service.

As a contingency against the failure of the Boot Server, copies of the programs for the most important small servers are kept in the filing systems of a number of free standing machines. If one of the servers fails and has to be reloaded, this can be done by running the Z80LOAD program on one of these machines. This process is not automatic, as it is when the Boot Server is operational, but it is sufficient to allow recovery of the system by manual intervention.

5.5 Remote debugging

SBOOT contains a simple debugging control routine designed to act as the agent of a more powerful debugging system running on another machine. The debugging system is normally used during the development of new services; programs that are regarded as being in service are not in dialogue with a debugging control routine per se, but, if they suffer a software failure which leads to an entry into the debugger, they contact a simple failure recording service before reloading.

The SBOOT debugging control routine can be entered voluntarily by the program running in a server. Additionally, each location in the memory of a server is initialised to a value which, if executed as an instruction, causes an entry into the debugging routine so that runaway execution will be trapped. Hardware stack overflow and underflow also provoke entry to the debugging control routine.

Sometimes it is necessary to force the program in a small server to enter the SBOOT debugging control routine so that the remote debugger can regain control over the server. This is done by arranging that the Ring software used by SBOOT recognises a special **interrupt minipacket** that contains a bit pattern which distinguishes it from header minipackets in the packet protocol. If the Ring driving routines in SBOOT observe such a minipacket, control is immediately diverted into the SBOOT debugging control routine. The special interrupt minipacket is not accepted from arbitrary machines, otherwise it would be possible for any user to cause a server to enter its debugger and corrupt its program. The restriction is that the interrupt minipacket must come from the Name Server machine (which has a fixed Ring station number that can be put into the SBOOT ROM). The Name Server machine provides a service called 'Z80INT' which can be asked to send an interrupt minipacket to a nominated server. In the present implementation, Z80INT makes no checks on the use of its service, and anyone can interrupt a machine. In a more protected system it would be necessary to arrange that Z80INT has access to a table of who was allowed to reset particular machines and to require that requests to it were authenticated using the mechanisms described in Chapter Nine.

The interrupt minipacket scheme is not foolproof because a program stuck in a loop, not polling the Ring, will ignore them. In such an eventuality the machine has to be interrupted by hand. The additional complexity of some sort of watchdog scheme was considered, but was not thought to be worth the small extra gain and, furthermore, it is not apparent how to make a device that is capable of detecting every conceivable sort of program failure.

The only other way to enter the SBOOT debugging control routine is by depressing a switch on the server which causes a 'non-maskable interrupt'. This switch is used as a last resort if the program in a server goes completely out of control.

The address of the remote debugging service is set up whenever a server is loaded from one of the results returned in response to the loading request. SBOOT remembers this address for use when its debugging control program is entered for the first time. The registers of the server are saved on entry to the control program, together with all of the system variables which the routine might alter, so that it is possible to restore the machine state on exit from the debugging routine. The first action of the debugging control routine is to send a message to the debugging service using the single shot protocol. The remote debugging program running sends back a reply packet containing a command for the debugging control routine in SBOOT. When this command has been processed, the debugging control routine sends a further request to the remote program. This new request contains the result, if any, of the last command. The remote program must then reply with the next command to be obeyed by SBOOT. If at any time this simple dialogue breaks down, the debugging session is abandoned by SBOOT and the program loading routine invoked so as to reload the machine. In this way a small server does not wait indefinitely if the remote debugging program loses contact, but reloads itself from the Boot Server if possible and resumes ordinary operation.

The permitted commands to the debugging control routine in SBOOT are as follows:

—read memory location
—write memory location
—resume execution
—change debugging service port number

These primitives are sufficient for the remote debugging program to control the server and provide the substrate upon which more powerful operations such as break-pointing can be erected.

When describing the program loading system, it was explained how the Z80LOAD program could be used to load programs into servers. In addition to specifying the bootstrap file name and machine to load as parameters, the name of a computer on which the remote debugger is running can be given. All machines that can run a remote debugging program have a name 'Z80DEB-X' in the Name Server, where 'X' is the name of the machine. Thus a command of the form below:

'Z80LOAD MACHINE=PRINTER FILE=.code DEBUG=ALPHA'

causes the file '.code' to be loaded into the server called 'PRINTER'. The Z80LOAD program looks up the name of the debugging service, 'Z80DEB-ALPHA' in this example, and includes the result with the loading data sent to the machine PRINTER. When the loaded program first enters the SBOOT debugger, either by a programmed entry or as the result of receiving an interrupt minipacket, the SBOOT debugging control routine tries to contact the debugging service at the address corresponding to 'Z80DEB-ALPHA'.

The standard remote debugging program is called 'Z80DEB' and reads the name of the machine to be debugged as a parameter. Z80DEB waits to receive a request from that machine. If need be, Z80DEB can send a request off to the Z80INT service so that an interrupt minipacket is directed to the server in order to secure its attention. The first command executed by Z80DEB is one to change the port number to which SBOOT should send debug request packets from there on. This is so that the standard port associated with the 'Z80DEB-X' service on the machine could be made free for use by another activation of Z80DEB. This allows several activations of the Z80DEB program to run in parallel on the same machine; this is very useful if a number of small servers are being debugged simultaneously.

When a debugging session is over, the programmer may leave the server running or he can cause it to be reloaded with some other program. If the server is left running and enters the SBOOT debugging routine subsequently, it tries to contact the debugging service set up when the machine was last loaded. If the remote debugging program is no longer in operation, no contact is made and SBOOT goes into its program loading routine to try to obtain a new program to run.

For services in every day use it is not generally useful to load them with a remote debugger set up. However, it is convenient to be able to record some information if such a server does suffer a failure taking it in to the SBOOT debugging routine. Therefore, by default, when programs are loaded from the Boot Server, the debugging service address points to a service called 'Z80DUMP'. This service simply extracts a dump of the registers of the machine and the SBOOT debugger entry reason. Z80DUMP is, for convenience, run on the same machine as the Boot Server and directs its output to the **Logger** for printing (see Section 6.3) and subsequent examination. Once the information has been recorded, Z80DUMP causes the program loading routine to be entered so that the server will be reloaded and the service resumed. There is a simple algorithm to prevent a persistent failure from provoking a continuous cycle of loading and dumping: the rule is to refrain from reloading a server if it calls Z80DUMP twice within one minute.

5.6 The Boot Server

The functions of the Boot Server are currently provided by a PDP-11/45 running the RSX-11M operating system. The bootstrap memory images for the servers are kept on discs local to the PDP-11/45 system so that the Boot Server is only dependent upon the Name Server. It is an essential requirement that the Boot Server can be reloaded and manipulated without the assistance of any other Ring services, otherwise it would be impossible to restart the whole distributed system after a total shutdown.

The Boot Server provides several commands that are used to control bootstrap files and to interact with servers. A programmer gives commands to the Boot Server by connecting a virtual terminal stream to the Boot Server and interacting with a simple command line interpreter.

Control over who is allowed to install or change services is under the jurisdiction of the Boot Server and use can be made of the user authentication system described in Chapter Nine to protect services from interference. Since the authentication system is based on a number of small servers, it is necessary that the Boot Server has a directly attached terminal at which commands can be given without the need for authentication, or with independent, local authentication.

There are commands to install new versions of services, to back up to an earlier version and to delete services. Servers can be remotely reloaded[1] when it is desired to put a new version into service. There is a command to determine details about bootstrap files, such as module names, by interrogating special information records in the files. Another command allows a specified bootstrap file to be loaded into any machine. This is useful for hardware test programs that are left in the Boot Server, not bound to any machine in particular, ready to be loaded when required.

5.7 Small server software

The small servers are programmed either in assembly code, using a locally written assembler, or in ALGOL68C[2]. In both cases, programs are cross-assembled or cross-compiled and modules linked together on some machine other than the server itself.

---

[1] This is done by sending a request to the Z80INT service.

[2] ALGOL68C is an extended subset of the language Algol 68, and was developed by another group in the Laboratory.

The earliest servers were written in assembly code because the ALGOL68C system was not available at the time. Since the introduction of the latter system it has been used for writing most new services and the influence of a powerful, type checked language on programmer productivity has been beneficial. A considerable library of utility software and protocol packages has been developed for the servers. The library is written in assembly code in order to minimise the memory space it requires and also so that servers written in assembly code can use it. ALGOL68C programs access routines in the library through 'code sections' in programs, using a feature of the language which permits machine code to be incorporated into program text. Typically a code section is embedded in a procedure with the same name as the assembler subroutine being used. The code section picks up the parameters of the procedure and loads them into registers before calling the subroutine. Results are passed back as the result of the ALGOL68C procedure containing the code section.

An outline description of a number of the major packages in the library is given below.

Packet Protocol Package. SBOOT contains routines for transmitting packets (TXBLK) and receiving them (RXBLK) which are used by the loading and debugging routines. These routines are sufficiently general that they can be called by the program running in a server as well as by SBOOT itself. A packet protocol transfer is described by a small control block which specifies the address and size of the buffer for the data in question, together with addressing details. For transmission, the address takes the form of the destination station number and route minipacket for the packet to send. Reception control blocks indicate the port number on which data for the buffer should arrive and whether or not the port is reserved for use by a single station. In addition a number of control bits select the checksum algorithm to be used and the action to be performed when the transfer is complete.

Transmission of packets is very simple. TXBLK retries transmission of the header packet up to a limit which may be set by the program. If the header is not accepted within the limit, a return code indicating failure is given. Otherwise, the entire packet is despatched before the routine returns. Thus, the sending of minipackets is not usually overlapped with ordinary computation.

Reception is a little more complicated because of the need to have a number of reception requests outstanding in some circumstances, for example when a machine is supporting several transactions in parallel. The Ring access circuit for the server can be polled to see if a minipacket has arrived by inspecting a certain memory address. If a minipacket has turned up, the routine RXBLK should be called with a chain of control blocks passed as its argument. RXBLK reads the header and route minipackets of the incoming packet and searches the chain of control blocks to see if there is one that is suitable for receiving the incoming packet. If there is no suitable control block, the packet is discarded. Otherwise a packet is copied off the Ring in its entirety into the corresponding buffer and the checksum inspected for correctness. It is possible to set a marker bit in the control block to indicate that one field of the control block is the address of a subroutine that should be called when the packet arrives. Therefore, if the marker bit is set, RXBLK calls the subroutine before returning to the original caller. Usually such subroutines set flags in memory in order to signal to other parts of the program that the transfer is complete and the data are ready to be processed. In very simple services, it is sometimes the case that the subroutine can actually get on with the requested operation and send back a packet in reply using TXBLK. For these services, the program is a trivial loop that polls the Ring waiting for a minipacket to arrive and then calls RXBLK to take in a packet and deal with it, before resuming the polling cycle once more.

Coroutine Package. Systems based on polling are conveniently driven by a structure of coroutines. A package is accordingly provided to manage a circular chain of coroutines under the control of a simple coroutine coordinator. Normally each coroutine is associated with a separate parallel activity within a server. A coroutine retains control until it finds that it cannot make progress because an external device is not ready or data is wanted from the Ring, in which case the coroutine returns to the coroutine coordinator. Control is then passed on to the next coroutine in sequence. As the coordinator cycles around the coroutines, they each try to make progress and hand over control when they run out of work. By using shared memory locations as semaphores, coroutines can interlock with one another and synchronise with the subroutines called when packets are received.

This simple approach to concurrency works well in most cases, because none of the parallel activities in a simple service involve large amounts of computation and control returns to each coroutine in a very short time. It was not felt necessary to go to the expense of writing a multi-tasking system, mainly because of the memory space it would occupy, and because the simple scheme is good enough.

Single Shot Protocol Package. Single shot transactions are represented by a simple data structure known as a channel which holds information about the buffers for the request and reply packets, together with the address of the service to be called. There is a subroutine that sets up a channel and takes the name of the service to be called as a string of characters. The request packet is sent by calling a subroutine and then the channel is inspected at regular intervals to see if a reply has arrived, or to time out if there is no reply. Such an interface is well suited for use in a system based on the coroutine package because the system can proceed with other work while waiting for the reply. The subroutine that transmits a request packet automatically handles the allocation of a port number for the reply packet and the setting up of a reception request control block. The single shot protocol package keeps a chain of all reception control blocks and a polling subroutine has to be called at intervals to see if a packet addressed to any of the buffers can be received.

There is an additional subroutine in the package which is used to set up reception control blocks in order to receive single shot protocol requests. The reply to a request can be sent back by using TXBLK directly.

Byte Stream Protocol Package. Byte streams are also represented by data structures called channels. Subroutines exist for both setting up outgoing byte streams to a named service and for picking up incoming byte streams. Buffers and ports for the byte stream are allocated automatically, and the programmer need not concern himself with the details of the exchange of byte stream protocol signals around the Ring. However a polling subroutine should be called with reasonable frequency in order that incoming packets can be received and pending transmission packets sent. To transfer data along the byte stream there are subroutines for reading and writing individual bytes of data. These subroutines give a return code to indicate whether or not the byte stream is ready to transfer another byte. If it is not, the program should cycle, repeatedly calling the subroutine until the transfer is successful. Additionally, there are several other subroutines for closing down byte stream connections, dealing with various error conditions and forcing the transmission of buffered material. Here again the subroutines making up the package are designed with the coroutine polling system in mind.

6 Simple Services

6.1 Introduction

This chapter describes several of the services that run on small servers. Others are described in the following chapters dealing with the Processor Bank and the authentication system.

6.2 The Name Server

The Name Server is the most fundamental of all of the services provided by the distributed system. Its function is that of name look up; that is, the translation from textual names of services and machines into numeric values. Machines are identified by the Ring station to which they are attached. This connection is not necessarily permanent; a machine may be physically moved to some other location, or stations may be renumbered for administrative reasons. Therefore, the binding of machines to Ring station numbers is not fixed, but must instead be discovered by asking the Name Server.

The Name Server is different from all the other small services in that it cannot be loaded from the Boot Server, because the loading system depends upon the Name Server for its operation. To deal with this, the Name Server program is kept in ROM so that it will not be destroyed if the machine loses power. There is also an initial name table in the ROM. The whole name table is kept on the File Server (see Chapter Four) and is read in by the Name Server when it is powered on. Thus, the name table in ROM must contain at least the name of the File Server. If the Name Server is unable to contact the File Server, it runs using the table held in ROM until the File Server responds. This table contains sufficient names to enable a restart of the major system services from cold.

Every machine in the network has a name, distinct from the name of any other machine or service. If this name is presented to the Name Server name look up service, using the single shot protocol, the eight bit number of the station to which the machine is currently attached will be returned. The address of the name look up service is fixed and cannot be varied, so that it may be safely written into programs. To find out the location of a particular service rather than a machine, it is necessary to find out:

a) on which machine the service is running

b) the port to which requests should be sent

c) for some protocols, a function code to indicate the service required.

The use made of port numbers (in route minipackets) and function codes varies from service to service. In general, port numbers are used to direct packets into appropriate buffers in a machine and function numbers are used to decide how to process the contents of a buffer. If a machine provides only a few services, it can allocate a buffer to each service and the port number alone is sufficient to decide what service is required when a request arrives. If a machine provides many services, it will probably only have as many buffers available as it is able to support concurrent activities, and function numbers will be used to select a particular service when a request arrives at any of the 'general enquiry' ports.

The Name Server supplies an indication of the protocol associated with a service when its name is looked up. This information is used by some operating systems to reject attempts by programs to use an inappropriate protocol when calling upon a service.

Textual names have no structure as far as the Name Server is concerned, but are treated as arbitrary character strings within a restricted alphabet so that structure can be added later. However, for convenience, services that are provided by many machines, the 'GIVEFILE' file transfer operation for example, take the form of a service component and a machine name. For example, the string 'GIVEFILE-BRAVO' is the name of the GIVEFILE service on the machine BRAVO. Thus programs that drive common services can easily manufacture the service name, given the name of the target machine.

To facilitate future developments in internetworking, in addition to returning a local Ring address in response to name lookup, the Name Server also returns a string. For local services, this string is null. For remote service, if a non-null string is returned, the string should be passed onto the next stage of communication for interpretation. Thus, local names for remote services may map onto the Ring address of a gateway which will use the string returned by the Name Server to set up communication paths in the internetwork.

The function of the Name Server is purely that of name look up, and it does not offer any guidance on whether or not a service is actually running. Thus the presence of an entry in the name table only determines where the service will run on those occasions when it is offered.

The Name Server has a reverse name look up service which will translate a station number into a textual name. This service is used if a computer wishes to report the identity of one of its clients in a readable way. There is a 'who am I?' service which reflects the fact that it is impossible for a machine to discover directly the number of the station to which it is attached. The service responds with the textual name of the machine making the request. If need be, this can be looked up to determine the actual station number.

From time to time new services have to be inserted into the name table and existing service names moved or deleted. Obviously, operations of this sort must be protected. At present the scheme is very simple: a machine can only alter the names of services it provides itself. There are two single shot protocol based Name Server operations, <u>add name</u> and <u>delete name</u>, that are used to put a name into the name table and delete a name from the table respectively. The restrictions on the use of the add name service do not prevent a programmer installing a name that is either pre-emptive, misleading or obscene for a service on his machine. In general, this problem cannot be solved without human intervention at some stage when new names are to be installed. In a more powerful name server it could be arranged that new names have to be vetted unless all of their components are standard. This would mean that there would be no difficulty in adding a name such as 'GIVEFILE-DELTA', but a more novel name would have to be approved first.

The restriction that names have to be changed from the machine to which they point is inconvenient, especially if the machine is a small server. It is also a great nuisance if many names have to be changed because a machine has been attached to a different station, or if the name table on the File Server is to be compacted or sorted. In these circumstances a modified name table may be generated as follows: a copy of the Name Server program with the restrictions on <u>add name</u> and <u>delete name</u> removed is loaded into a spare small server; this version of the Name Server program reads down the name table from the File Server. Like the real Name Server, the version running in the spare machine updates the File Server copy of the name table in response to add name and delete name requests. In this way a new name table is built up in the File Server. If the real Name Server is then restarted, it will take the new table and use it in normal operation. This rather primitive scheme could be improved upon if the Name Server made use of the interlocks on files provided by the File Server so that updates to the name table from the main Name Server were locked out while a new table is being generated. At present, any such update is lost but since names are not added very often this is not a problem in practice.

There is a service provided by the Name Server that can be used by any machine to generate a list of the entries in the name table. This service is used mainly to automate the production of an up-to-date printed list of all the services and their locations for reference purposes. The service is also used by the program that drives the unrestricted Name Server when a new name table is to be set up in order to discover the current contents of the table. Like all Name Server operations, this service is implemented using the single shot protocol. Each call contains an entry number and the Name Server replies with a copy of the data in that entry of the name table. The name table is represented as a vector of entries. When an entry beyond the end of the vector is requested a dummy terminating entry will be returned so that it may be determined when all of the table has been read out. In addition to details about an entry, the name listing service also returns a name table version number so that a program scanning the table can detect changes taking place during the course of the scan.

The important role played by the Name Server in the distributed system makes its continued operation of paramount importance. In practice, the small server hardware, upon which the Name Server is based, is very reliable with no failure of the Name Server having been recorded in over two years of operation.

6.3 Time Server and Logger

The **Time Server** is used as a central source of local date and time information. The machine on which it runs is connected to a simple radio receiver that picks up 60 kHz time signals emitted by the MSF transmitter at Rugby, England. The Time Server has a timing circuit driven by the clock oscillator for the processor chip. Interrupts from this timing circuit are used to determine time intervals. In parallel, signals from the radio are monitored and put to a number of integrity checks because the radio channel is subject to considerable noise within the Computer Laboratory. Correctly received signals are used to resynchronise the time computed on the basis of the local oscillator. It is essential that the Time Server should be able to run in the absence of the radio signal, because the transmitter is turned off for several hours from time to time in order to carry out maintenance work. The Time Server is tuned to be as accurate as possible in the absence of a radio signal. It will, therefore, never have to change the time very much when the radio signal is resumed, but the change could be a short step backwards. This feature renders the present Time Server implementation unsuited to synchronisation and timestamping; were this desired, it would be necessary to arrange that in the absence of a radio signal the Time Server was slightly slow.

The Time Server provides two services: 'DAT' for date and time information and 'CLOCK' which sends off packets at regular intervals. Both services are implemented in terms of the single shot protocol.

The DAT service returns an indication of the current date and time to a resolution of one second. The date is represented in numeric form so that it can be used directly for calculations. The format is straightforward and can be readily converted to a textual form suitable for display. The DAT service is used by some machines to set clocks in their operating systems running from the correct initial value. In particular, the TRIPOS operating system when run on a processing server starts its clock in this way.

The CLOCK service is intended for machines that do not have an internal clock and require regular time signals. The initial request to the CLOCK service specifies what the frequency of signalling is to be, in the range one to 255 seconds. Each packet sent by the CLOCK service is directed to a reply port specified in the initial request. Each packet sent contains full date and time information together with a sequence number so that the client can detect lost packets easily.

The machine that supports the DAT and CLOCK services has a teletypewriter attached to it and provides a logging service, referred to below as the **Logger**. The logging service has the name 'WTO-LOG' and it prints out textual messages sent as strings of characters in single shot requests. The printed message is accompanied by a timestamp derived from the Time Server. The logging service is used mainly to keep a record of significant events which may be useful during fault finding. For example, the Boot Server logs machines loaded after being reset and the Z80DUMP service sends a record of small server crashes to the log. Additionally, the Processor Bank management system notes the failure of any of its machines or services. WTO-LOG is a particular example of a general WTO (Write To Operator) service provided by many machines as a way of sending short textual messages across the Ring for the attention of the operator or operating system of a machine.

The Logger tries to detect Ring failures and to record when machines are turned off and on. Once a second or so the Logger sends a minipacket to every station. If a minipacket comes back marked as accepted, busy or unselected, the addressed machine is assumed to be powered on. If the ignored response is obtained, either there is no such station, or else it has been switched off. From this information it is possible to deduce when machines are turned off and on. These events are printed and timestamped. The Logger attempts to give machine names, if possible, by using the Name Server. If the Name Server does not reply, machine station numbers are printed so that the log will still contain useful information even if the Name Server has been lost.

6.4 Error Reporter

One of the notable features of the Cambridge Ring is the level of self checking carried out by Ring stations. If a station detects an error such as a loss of framing, modulation failure, data corruption and so forth, a special maintenance minipacket is sent to station number zero at the first opportunity. On the current Ring station zero is connected to a dedicated machine, based upon the small server hardware and known as the Error Reporter, which keeps a record of the errors and prints them out on a teletypewriter. The program in the Error Reporter is kept in ROM so that the logging remains operational even if none of the standard services are available, as might be the case on a small development Ring, or if there are errors disrupting normal use of the Ring. New versions of the program can be tested using the small server software development system and need only be fixed in ROM when they have been thoroughly tested.

The Error Reporter prints out an immediate record, timestamped if possible, of errors when they occur. It also accumulates error totals over a twenty four hour period. The Error Reporter attempts to obtain the current time from the Time Server. If the Time Server is not accessible, an internal cycle count is printed and this can be used to estimate the time between errors.

For much of the time the Ring makes very few errors and it is useful to have a machine recording any that do arise and at what time. If there is a break in the Ring, the next station down stream from the broken link will send maintenance minipackets to station zero where they will be logged and can be interpreted by an engineer in order to locate the break. The Error Reporter will produce a compressed report when there is a severe failure or if the Ring becomes disconnected, so that helpful information will not be swamped by a flood of error messages.

6.5 Pointing Machine Server

The Computer Laboratory has a semi-automatic wire-wrap machine, usually referred to as the pointing machine from its mode of operation. It consists of a table onto which a circuit board may be fixed and a head which is moved over the table by a pair of stepping motors. The machine is driven so that the head moves from pin to pin across the circuit board. At each pin the operator rests a wire-wrapping tool on the head to make a connection. There are a number of lamps which are used to signal to the operator and there are some buttons which may be pressed to indicate such things as completion of a wrap, the need to repeat one, and so forth. A teletypewriter attached to the server is used to give instructions to the operator and to provide a means by which the operator can communicate with the machine sending commands. The pointing machine is attached to the Ring via a standard small server.

There is a program which takes a description of a circuit, in terms of the location of the components and the interconnections between them, and constructs a wiring schedule for the pointing machine. The output of this program is a series of coordinates to be joined with an indication of the length and colour of wire to use. The wiring schedule is annotated with a description of each connection referring to the names of circuits used when the schedule was generated.

The code required to interpret a wiring schedule is fairly large and, in consequence, a more powerful computer than a simple microprocessor is required. The program is run on a computer in the Processor Bank on those occasions when the pointing machine is in use. This avoids dedicating a big machine to be the pointing machine server all of the time. The small amount of code needed in the small server interfacing the pointing machine to the Ring is very simple. The division of responsibility between the small program in the microcomputer and the more complex program running in a processing server has the great benefit that the latter could be developed within the framework of the TRIPOS operating system, which provides a greater range of programming tools than the small server software system.

The driving program has a byte stream connection with the server. The driving program sends coordinates to the server, patterns to set on the lamps and messages for the teletypewriter. The server uses the byte stream to send signals back to the driving program when the head has been positioned, buttons are pressed, and when the operator types on the keyboard. The protocol between the server and the driving program is designed to make it easy for the latter to keep a record of how much of the schedule has been completed so that the operator could stop one job part way through in order to give precedence to another job.

The normal mode of operation of the Pointing Machine Server is for the operator to type a start up message on the keyboard giving the file name of the wiring schedule for the current job. The Pointing Machine Server then contacts the **Resource Manager** (see Section 8.1) to obtain a processing server to run the driving program. Once the processing server makes contact, the operator can start receiving instructions about the connections to be made.

6.6 Terminal Concentrators

A number of small servers have been built to act as Terminal Concentrators, connecting up to eight terminal lines to the Ring at standard rates up to 19200 baud. Terminal communication is conducted using the **virtual terminal protocol** which is built on top of the byte stream protocol. Every terminal connection is represented as a separate byte stream to the host computer and there is no multiplexing of connections down a single byte stream.

There are a number of conflicting requirements for a Terminal Concentrator. For many machines it is useful to have the Concentrator deal with keyboard echoing and line editing locally so that the host is presented with lines of input ready for use, with no further processing needed. On the other hand, there are programs such as screen editors that wish to make their own interpretation of keystrokes and do not require any action in the Concentrator. The virtual terminal protocol provides for this by allowing each request for an input record to specify how the Concentrator is to act in terms of a series of attributes. The various possibilities are listed below as independent pairs of mutually exclusive options:

1 Local echoing of keystrokes by the Concentrator
2 No echoing of keystrokes by the Concentrator
3 Interpret line editing functions such as rubout;

treat carriage return (and certain other keystrokes) as record terminators

4 No line editing or record terminators; records are only terminated when completely filled

5 Interpret escape sequences for non-standard characters

6 No interpretation of escape sequences

7 Terminate records on any control character (in addition to either option 3 or 4)

8 Treat all control characters (except those used by option 3, if selected) as data characters within a record

Attributes 1, 3, and 5 - keystroke echoing and full line editing - are those used by programs that want a simple line-by-line interface to the terminal. Options 2, 4 and 6 - no interpretation of characters - are intended for programs like screen editors. Such programs normally ask for one character at the time. However, if the host had fallen behind the Concentrator, the response is a record containing a number of characters which the host can process forthwith and catch up without making any further requests. If the host is keeping up with the Concentrator, responses will contain only single characters.

The seventh option, which selects transmission of buffered keystrokes on control characters, is used by hosts that strip off control characters in their terminal driving programs and use them to switch the terminal stream between tasks or generate end of file marks and so forth. If it is desired to pass one of the control characters through as data, an escape sequence must be typed on the terminal since typing the character itself will cause it to be taken as a control character.

The remarks about control characters illustrate one of the problems with virtual terminal systems and that is that the user has to be aware, potentially, of three levels of terminal handling: the Concentrator, the terminal driving software of the host and the program to which input is directed. In general terms, it is much simpler if the terminal driving code in the host relies entirely upon the facilities of the Concentrator and does not steal extra codes for its own purposes. Otherwise there will be gratuitous differences between terminal conventions on different machines and confusion will result.

Output is much simpler than input. The host sends a complete record of characters to the Concentrator together with an indication of how the record should be terminated. The record is then displayed on the terminal. The present implementation of the Terminal Concentrator does not have facilities for local interpretation of control characters such as those for tabulation on output.

Interactions with the Terminal Concentrator are fully duplex and it is the responsibility of the host to deal with any synchronisation that is required. The Concentrator buffers keystrokes that arrive before an input line request is received and only interprets them when a request is available and the options are known. Escape sequences are used to generate codes that do not correspond to any key, to switch reflection off and on locally and to generate end of logical stream markers.

The user can talk directly to the Terminal Concentrator by pressing the break key. All further characters are interpreted by the Concentrator and commands can be given to switch between connections, make new connections, disconnect streams and to transmit byte stream resets to hosts. When a byte stream reset occurs, the host and the Concentrator may exchange codes either admitting to being responsible for the reset or denying responsibility. The reset will be denied by both ends if it was invoked to resynchronise after protocol errors. The Concentrator takes no special action when the host admits to causing a reset. A reset provoked by the Concentrator is interpreted by the host as a break signal to gain the attention of its operating system.

The flow of data between host and Concentrator is structured as a simple stream of bytes. Ordinary characters are represented by values in the range 0-127. Values in the range 128-255 are used as markers for record boundaries and control information passing across the stream. On input, there is a special control marker which indicates that the next byte is not to be interpreted as a control byte, thereby giving a mechanism to pass any value in the range 0-255 as a character. It is an omission of the protocol that only values in the range 0-127 may occur in records for output.

Terminal connections are made by giving the Terminal Concentrator the name of the service or machine to connect to. This name is transformed into a string of the form 'RATS-X' where 'X' is the name of the service or machine. ('RATS' is an acronym for Remotely Activated Terminal Session.) The Concentrator will look up the string in the Name Server and attempt to open a byte stream to the address returned by the Name Server. If the byte stream is established successfully, virtual terminal protocol transactions will take place across the stream for as long as the connection persists. A connection may be abandoned either by the host closing the byte stream, after a 'FINISH' command for example, or by a command to the Concentrator issued by the user.

6.7 Printer Server

The Printer Server is connected to both a lineprinter and a daisy-wheel printer. Byte stream connections can be made to the server for sending documents to either device, although only one document is accepted at a time for each device. It is left to the clients of the server to do their own spooling of material if they find the server busy printing for someone else. There are buttons associated with the printer that can be pressed by an operator to indicate that the current document should be repeated after a paper jam or that it should be abandoned, for example if the output is nonsensical. In the event of such an action, the byte stream is reset and a code indicating the reason for the reset sent back to the client before the stream is closed down by the Printer Server. It is the responsibility of the client machine to interpret the reason for the reset and repeat the printing of the document if appropriate.

6.8 Other applications

The presence of a number of uncommitted small machines attached to the network is extremely useful for conducting experiments and making low cost temporary interfaces to the Ring for a variety of equipment. Some examples are described below.

Terminal Adaptors. A simple gateway for connecting terminals on Ring Terminal Concentrators to the British Telecom Packet Switched System (PSS) network is implemented as a small server connected to a serial data line from a PSS network node. The server accepts virtual terminal connections and copies data in both directions between the Ring and PSS.

A similar technique could be used to provide access from the Terminal Concentrators to a machine that does not support the virtual terminal protocol, with a small server acting as an adaptor to connect terminal lines from the machine to the Ring. This is primarily appropriate when software is being developed for new machines and there is no suitable Ring software or even no Ring connection immediately to hand.

Hardware Development. During the commissioning of a version of the Ring implemented on gate array chips and during the testing of the Ring interfaces for machines in the Processor Bank small servers have been employed as programmable testbeds. The machines generated test patterns of signals for the chips and monitored the results.

One small server is attached to a PROM blowing circuit and is used to change the PROMs found in various Ring interfaces and the PROMs in small servers, holding the SBOOT control program. The new contents of the PROM are sent using the single shot protocol. The server copies the data into the PROM and checks that the operation has been successful by reading back the contents.

In the area of measurement, small servers have been connected to various sorts of monitors and counters in order to analyse traffic patterns on the Ring and to calculate usage statistics.

Digital Voice. In a project to handle real-time digitised voice over the Ring, small servers interface telephones to the system and provide a dialling and connection service for routing calls.

Protocol Development. During the development of the Ring protocols, small servers have been used as sinks and sources of data, and as 'mirrors' that bounce back the data sent to them. For the testing of the byte stream protocol, a mirror was written that would occasionally corrupt the data sent to it so that the error recovery aspects of the protocol could be investigated.

7 The Processor Bank

7.1 Processing servers

This chapter is concerned with aspects of the Processor Bank in terms of the facilities provided for the use of processing servers. Central to the concept of using a remotely located machine as a personal computer is the need to exercise complete control over it. In the Cambridge Distributed System this is achieved by incorporating control functions into the Ring interfaces for processing servers. The following sections describe the Ring interface for LSI4 minicomputers, the functions of the Ancilla and the control facilities provided. During early stages of the project, the processing servers were all Computer Automation LSI4 16-bit minicomputers, each with 64K words of memory and the Processor Bank comprised nine of these machines. More recently seven further processing servers based on the Motorola 68000 microprocessor with 256K bytes of memory[1] have been installed in the Processor Bank. The ensuing description of the Processor Bank will be given only in terms of the LSI4 minicomputers as the organisation and management for both sorts of machine is essentially identical. However the fact that two completely different families of computers can coexist in the Processor Bank demonstrates the success of the Cambridge Distributed System approach to the organisation of a collection of heterogeneous machines.

----

[1] The standard memory circuit card for the system can accommodate up to 512K bytes and it is expected that the machines will be upgraded in the fullness of time.

In principle, the LSI4s have no peripherals apart from a Ring interface which will be described fully in the next section. However to facilitate stand-alone operation of the machines for maintenance, there is a serial character I/O board and a floppy disc system that can be put onto a machine if need be.

The LSI4 has a reasonable and extensive instruction set. It is an adequate machine for running a single user operating system and supporting high-level languages. An important property of the LSI4 is that it has no memory mapping hardware, limiting the addressable memory capacity to 64K words. In a larger version of the distributed system, machines of the size of the LSI4 would be amongst the smallest in the Processor Bank and there would be other more powerful machines with faster processors and larger memories.

7.2 Processor Bank Ring interfaces

The Ring interface for the LSI4 computers has much more to do than just provide the machines with access to the Ring, because they are located at some distance from their users and have to be controlled remotely. With a personal computer, a user expects to use some form of control panel to start his machine, stop it, and bootstrap code into its memory. Bootstrapping is often done by interacting with a simple control program that calls down memory images from a local disc. For a processing server, the Ring interface must provide a similar degree of control over the machine, accepting commands from across the Ring. This leads to integrity problems associated with preventing one user from taking over control of a machine owned by another.

The Ring interface for a processing server is its only access to other services; in particular, all files must be accessed through the File Server because the processing server cannot have a local filing system in the way that a personal computer does. In consequence there is a strong requirement that the access circuit function of the interface should offer high performance in terms of data transfer rates. This is interpreted as the need to implement the packet protocol in the interface using direct memory access (DMA) to transfer data between the Ring and the memory of the server without the involvement of the server's central processor.

There are a number of benefits that come from connecting machines to a network using powerful interfaces. Firstly, the program in the interface is more secure than software put into the machine itself. There is no risk of the code in the interface being accidentally overwritten, or of the interface losing control over the machine. Secondly, the interface contains a fixed program that cannot be corrupted by the user of the machine and in consequence the interface can be trusted by the Processor Bank management system. This point is of crucial importance: it is our view that there should be no restrictions made upon the software that can be loaded into a processing server so that programmers can develop their own operating systems and application programs at will. In other words, processing servers, when on loan to a user, should be exactly like personal computers.

It is important that the Ring interface is not too complicated, otherwise its cost would be unduly high, especially for smaller machines. The interface to be described subsequently is comparable in cost and complexity to a simple disc controller for a modern minicomputer. To reduce the amount of programming required for the interfaces, they do the bare minimum necessary to support remote control and there is a special server, called the **Ancilla** (Latin: housemaid), devoted to supporting the Ring interfaces and providing high level operations for other machines to use. The advantage of this approach is that changes in the arrangements for controlling processing servers can, in general, be achieved by modifying the Ancilla alone, leaving the programs in the interfaces unaltered. where the number of interfaces will be large and making a change to all of them would be very inconvenient.

Another feature of the Ancilla is that it can conceal low level differences between interfaces for different sorts of processing server and present a uniform, machine independent, set of functions to its clients.

7.3 Ring interface design

The processing server Ring interface is designed as a general interface suitable for most 16-bit minicomputers and is based on the Signetics 8X300 microprocessor. This is a fast bipolar technology device optimised for use in high speed applications. It has a simple instruction set which is designed for shifting and merging eight bit data items. There are also instructions for testing a combination of bits in a byte and branching on the result. The clock cycle time for a single instruction is 250 ns. The program for the 8X300 is held in 2K bytes of fast ROM and there are 256 bytes of RAM for use as workspace.

The 8X300 is surrounded by a variety of support circuits for handling Ring reception, Ring transmission, DMA read, DMA write and DMA addressing. Both the Ring logic and the DMA logic is bi-directional so that transmission and reception may take place simultaneously. All of the data paths go through the microprocessor rather than being directly connected. This is because the operations of computing checksums and the rules for retransmitting minipackets were thought to be too complex for implementation in hardware alone. The address buffers used by the DMA interface are arranged to be auto-incrementing in order to speed up memory access times.

To make the interface host independent, so that it will be suitable for a variety of 16-bit minicomputers, it is logically and physically split into two parts as shown in the diagram below. The first part contains the 8X300 processor and the Ring access circuit; the second is simply the mechanism needed to operate the host machine's bus, and to perform basic DMA operations. The interface between these halves is an idealised set of DMA signals: address bus, data bus, DMA request and acknowledge lines. A consequence of this split in the design is that the program for the 8X300 is host independent since it works in terms of the idealised interface.

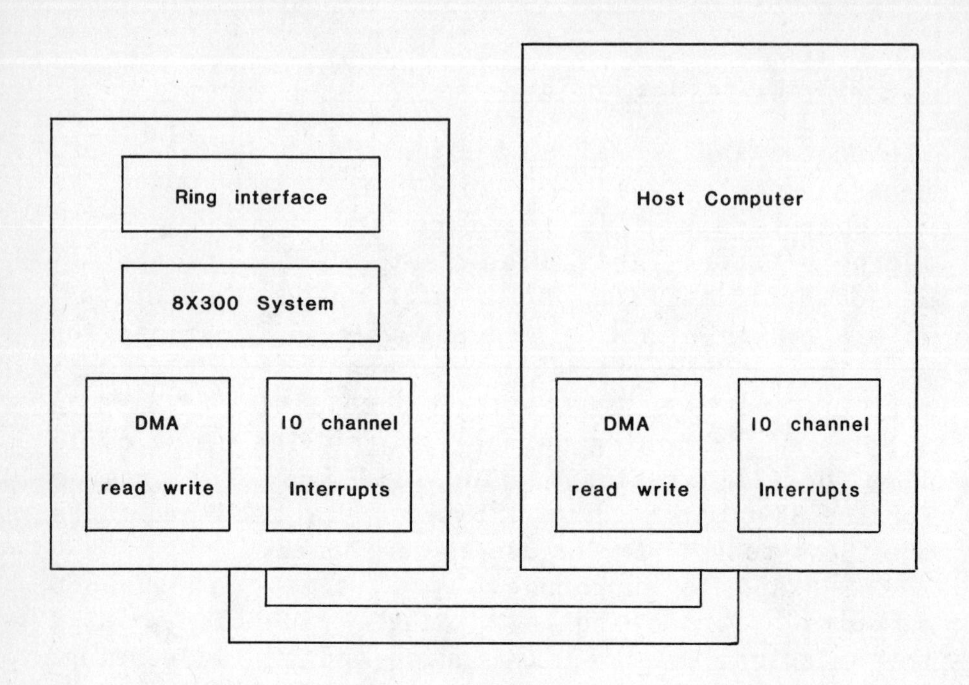

The processor and Ring interface is fabricated as three printed circuit cards measuring approximately 7.5 inches square and designed to fit in the same racks as printed circuit board versions of Ring stations and repeaters. The first card contains the 8X300 processor and Ring access circuits, a total of about thirty five chips. The two other cards are the channels for DMA read and write operations respectively and each contain about thirty chips. These two cards are identical, except for a coding plug, and the overall design admits to the possibility of a system with just a single channel. The channel boards provide the idealised DMA interface which has to be mapped into the LSI4 DMA architecture. This is done by a further printed circuit board, designed to fit into an LSI4 chassis and holding just over fifty chips. All of the boards are interconnected by ribbon cables and the host interface board may be some short distance away from the others.

The hardware commissioning and software development for the interface made novel use of a Z80-based small server which acted as a support processor for the interface. In a normal interface, the program is held in fast ROM. For the commissioning system the ROM access logic was made to address part of the memory of a small server. Thus new programs could be loaded into the interface by updating the memory of the small server. The small server contained a simple loading and debugging package which could be driven from a remote machine by sending messages across the Ring. The remote machine ran a number of utility programs that interpreted commands from a terminal and translated them into messages to the small server to update the memory shared with the Ring interface. This configuration turned out to be very powerful and flexible both during the early testing of the hardware and later during development of the software to run in the interface.

In the light of recent developments in the microprocessors available commercially it is likely that it will become much easier to build interfaces of the sort just described. The development of the 8X300 system was a difficult project because of the number of circuits needed to drive the DMA interfaces and support the processor. Furthermore, the limited program memory space (2K words) and even smaller workspace (256 bytes) severely restricted the amount that can be done by the interface, particularly given the instruction set of the 8X300 which is not designed for this type of application. Most of the standard microprocessors based on MOS technology are too slow to drive the Ring directly, but a number of them are well provided with support circuits for handling DMA transfers. It would also be possible to speed things up further by using uncommitted logic arrays to implement circuits for checksum calculation and minipacket retransmission handling. Taken in conjunction with the better programming environment and larger memory space obtained by use of a MOS microprocessor, these factors could well lead to a different future design for processing server Ring interfaces. In particular an interface could take on some of the functions provided by the Ancilla, making the latter redundant. In the interests of flexibility, such an interface would only contain a small fixed stub of code to load the full interface software across the Ring in a fashion analogous to the operation of the small servers.

7.4 Loading and debugging

In addition to handling data transfer across the Ring, the interface has to provide the means by which a processing server is controlled remotely. There are two aspects to remote control: how does the interface distinguish requests directed to itself from the ordinary data transfers into the processing server, and how does the interface protect itself from accepting control commands from the wrong source?

The addressing problem is solved by using one of the four notionally spare bits in a route minipacket, the remaining twelve bits being a port number (see Section 3.3). If this bit is set in the route minipacket of an incoming packet, the contents of the packet are intercepted by the interface, rather than being copied into the processing server's memory.

The protection problem is solved by insisting that initiation of loading or debugging must come from the Ancilla. However it is not sufficient for the processing server Ring interface to look up a name like 'ANCILLA' in the Name Server, because in a heterogenous Processor Bank there will have to be a different Ancilla for each type of machine. The name of the Ancilla cannot be put into the Ring interface program, because the program is machine independent. Instead, it is necessary for the Ring interface to go to the **Resource Manager**, the server that oversees the Processor Bank, via the Name Server to find out the name of its Ancilla. The Resource Manager holds this information since it has to be able to tell the appropriate Ancilla to load a processing server when it is allocated.

In the present implementation a regrettable shortcut has been taken because of a lack of space in the Ring interface memory. The station number of the Ancilla is held on a coding plug in the interface itself. In future Ring interfaces, which will have more program space, the full transaction with the Resource Manager will be employed.

The Ring interface is set into a special loading mode by sending it a request packet. The interface abandons any work it is doing for the processing server and only accepts further loading commands from the Ancilla. The loading commands are sent as a series of individual packets addressed to a command port. The first data minipacket of each packet selects the command to be obeyed. The load command has two arguments: a loading pointer and a count. The load command packet should be followed by a train of packets addressed to a data port (different from the command port). The contents of these packets will be copied into the processing server's memory from the address given by the loading pointer onwards. The count parameter to the load command tells the interface how many words to expect. If another command is sent to the command port before the loading command has completed, loading is abandoned and the next command is processed normally. The start command allows the processing server to begin executing instructions; however, the interface will not respond to the processing server until an end command is given to resume normal operation. There is also a reset command which sets the interface back to the state it was in when it first entered the loading mode. The reset command is not restricted to use during loading mode only: it can be issued at any time and provides a convenient way to stop a processing server.

There are three commands for the remote debugging of processing servers and they are implemented as individual request packets. Before a remote debugging program can take control, a set debugger command must be sent from the Ancilla. This command has one argument, nominating the station from which future debugging commands are to be accepted. The Ancilla can cancel a debugging session by giving zero as the argument and the interface will accept no further commands until another set debugger command is issued with a non-zero station number as its argument. The commands for interrogating the processing server are read word and write word with the obvious interpretations. These primitives are very simple, but they are about the most general that can be provided if the debugging facilities are to be truly machine independent.

If a remote debugging program requires more powerful facilities, such as access to the processing server's registers, or break-pointing, it is necessary to have a small stub of a debugger resident in the processing server itself. The remote debugger can load this stub into the machine using the write word command and very simple communication between the stub and the remote program can be achieved by reading and writing data in the processing server's memory.

7.5 Packet protocol operations

A processing server presents commands for data transfers to its Ring interface by transmitting the address of a command vector as a single word transfer through an I/O port. The interface uses DMA to read the contents of the command vector, which may be several words long, and then acts upon the command it contains. Since the interface can multiplex several commands in parallel, commands may be satisfied in a different order to that in which they are submitted. The interface passes back information about a completed command by writing back the address of the corresponding command vector as a data transfer through an I/O port to the processing server. This transfer interrupts the processing server which should read the address of the command vector from the I/O port in order to discover the reason for the interrupt.

For transmission, a command vector describes the transmission of a single packet. The command vector indicates the destination station and the contents of the route minipacket. It also contains a descriptor of the buffer from which the data part of the packet should be read. The remaining fields of the command vector are a return code filled in by the interface when it has finished with the command vector and a series of option bits for indicating how the command vector should be interpreted. Transmission command vectors may be linked into a chain and the interface will pass down the chain transmitting each packet in turn. A bit in the options field is used to specify that an interrupt should be given when the packet described by the command vector has been transmitted. Thus a train of packets may be sent off with only a single interrupt to be generated at the end of the transfer. When the transfer is either completed or abandoned in the face of persistent rejection, the return code field is set to indicate the reason for finishing.

Reception is more complicated. As before, command vectors contain a buffer descriptor of where in the processing server's memory received data should be placed. A port number field is set up with the port number associated with the buffer and a station number field may be set either to select one station or to allow data to come from any station. There are option bits and a return code field, together with a count field which, after a transfer has been completed, indicates how many words were received into the buffer.

Command vectors specifying the same station and route combinations may be chained together. The interface will maintain different chains for each distinct station and route combination presented to it, so that several reception requests may be outstanding at one time. The rules for processing a chain are as follows: the first packet received is read into the first buffer on the chain until either the entire packet has been received, or the buffer is full. If the buffer is complete, the chain word is followed and the next buffer filled likewise. If the chain word is zero, a 'last command vector in chain' bit in the options field is inspected. If the bit is set and there is still data to come, the complete transfer is abandoned with an error indication. Normally this case will only arise if the transmitter has sent more data than was expected. As every packet is received, the options field of the command vector being processed at the time is inspected to see if an 'end of packet' interrupt should be generated. When a buffer is filled, the options field of the command vector is interrogated to see if an 'end of buffer' interrupt should be generated.

The 'return code' and 'words read' fields in the returned command vectors are updated so that the processing server may determine the fate of the transfer. The rules outlined above allow the host to set up a chain of command vectors to receive a succession of packets into a single buffer, or alternatively to break down a transfer into a series of buffers. The first feature, that of reading several packets into one buffer is particularly appropriate for driving the File Server protocols (see Chapter Four). If a processing server requests to read some part of a file, the File Server will send the data as a train of packets in quick succession until the transfer is complete. The data can be received by setting up a single command vector for a buffer as big as the amount of data expected with the 'end of buffer interrupt' option selected. The Ring interface will take in the packets as they arrive and only interrupt the processing server when the entire transfer is done. The ability to direct separate parts of a transfer to different buffers is useful for stripping of protocol headers from packets in the single shot and byte stream protocols.

An additional facility provided by the interface is the ability to cancel outstanding reception transfers. The command vector for this is very simple and contains the address of the command vector to be cancelled. It is not possible to cancel a command vector that is currently being executed.

Timeouts on transfers must be done by the processing server using its internal clock. Transmissions do not have to be timed because they are abandoned after a sufficient number of retries have failed. Timed out reception requests can be stopped by using the cancel operation.

7.6 The Ancilla

An Ancilla service is responsible for supporting the Ring interfaces for the processing servers in a Processor Bank. It provides the users of processing servers with a high level interface for exercising control over their machines. There will be a different Ancilla for each type of machine in the Processor Bank, because the way in which the processing servers are controlled at the lowest level is obviously machine dependent. In the model system, the Processor Bank consists of LSI4 minicomputers and microcomputer systems based on the Motorola 68000. There is an Ancilla service for each variety, provided by one of the small Z80-based servers of the sort described in Chapter Five.

The Ancilla accepts requests to load machines only from the Resource Manager (see Section 8.1). The Resource Manager will issue a loading request in response to a command from a user, asking for a machine to be allocated to him and specifying what is to be loaded. The source of a loading request is checked to be the Resource Manager by use of the Name Server reverse look up operation. The simplest way to identify what is to be loaded is to give the Ancilla a File Server PUID and it will copy the contents of the file into the memory of the processing server. This basic level of operation is well suited to loading sensitive programs which it would be dangerous to keep in a filing system accessible to others. For example, the File Server garbage collector (see Section 4.4) is invoked via the Resource Manager and the PUID for its code is only known to the File Server.

For more public files, such as the one for the TRIPOS operating system, it is less desirable that the file should be specified by its PUID. This is because knowledge of a File Server PUID permits any operation on a file, including overwriting it. Even if the File

Server were to be augmented with some sort of access control over files, for example different PUIDs permitting read and write access to files, it would not be possible to prevent copying of files unless there was some sort of load-only access status which would prevent the file being read by anything other than the Ancilla. Copying is dangerous because any protection checks made by the loaded system before it runs can be overwritten in the copy, giving an unprivileged user excessive powers. Similarly, without load-only protection, it would be possible to read a loading file and discover any secret File Server PUIDs or protection system keys contained within it.

The solution to these problems is to associate loading files with text names and keep them in a simple filing system which can apply any necessary access controls. This filing system can be part of the Resource Manager, in which case all communication with the Ancilla will be in terms of File Server PUIDs, or alternatively, the filing system can be part of the Ancilla. In the present system, the filing system resides with the Ancilla and the Resource Manager will allow loading files to be named by either a PUID or a text name, for passing directly to the Ancilla. The Ancilla's filing system makes use of the File Server for holding the loading files. Files can be created in the filing system by giving the Ancilla a text name for the file and passing over its PUID. Thus a loading file may be generated by running a suitable system generation program to set up the file in the user's filing system and subsequently to put it into the Ancilla's filing system by handing over its PUID, rather than by making a copy of it.

The present implementation of the Ancilla does not support a full set of filing system operations: the number of files is relatively static and corresponds to the set of standard public systems in everyday use.

The loading files are not simple memory images: a more compact representation is employed in the interests of disc space economy in the File Server. A loading file is laid out as a series of directives followed by the data to be loaded. The Ancilla scans the directives in sequence and maintains a loading pointer which indicates the next location of memory in the processing server to be written to, and a reading pointer which indicates the next word from the data part of the loading file to be copied into memory. Data is copied in response to the load directive which takes the number of words to copy as its argument. This directive causes both the loading pointer and the reading pointer to move forwards. Memory may be cleared by using the clear directive which has as its first argument the number of words of memory to be set to a value given by its second argument. This directive will only move the loading pointer. The remaining major directives for copying data are set loading pointer and stop loading. There are other machine dependent directives concerned with starting the loaded machine executing instructions. The Ancilla translates these directives into the low level operations supported by the processing server Ring interfaces, copying data from the File Server as need be.

7.7 TRIPOS for the processing servers

TRIPOS[2] is a portable operating system written in BCPL by a group at the Computer Laboratory led by Dr Martin Richards. TRIPOS is designed as a system to run on 16-bit minicomputers without memory mapping and is therefore well suited to the LSI4 computers in the Processor Bank. It is a stand-alone, single user system and expects to have access to a local disc for its filing system and a directly attached terminal. TRIPOS has two facets. In one respect it is a real-time operating system kernel and set of device driving routines. Its other aspect is that of a personal computer operating system because a large number of utility programs such as command language interpreters, editors, compilers and debuggers have

---

[2] M. Richards, A.R. Aylward, P. Bond, R.D. Evans and B.J. Knight. September 1979. 'TRIPOS - a portable operating system for minicomputers'. Software - Practice and Experience, 9.

been produced for it. An intended use of TRIPOS is that when a project is to be started on a new machine, one should first bring up the operating system on that machine and then use the system and its utilities to develop the application program. The File Server was developed in this way and retains the structure of the TRIPOS kernel at the heart of its code. TRIPOS is thoroughly oriented towards the language BCPL and in some sense may be thought of as a multi-tasking BCPL runtime system, although there are compilers and language libraries for Pascal, Fortran and ALGOL68C. All of the TRIPOS system itself is written in BCPL with the exception of the multi-tasking coordinator and lowest level device driving routines which are written in assembly code. When TRIPOS is to be moved to a new machine, the assembly code routines have to be rewritten and a BCPL code generator for the new machine is required. To transfer TRIPOS to a new machine from scratch takes about six man-months.

Communication between processes or <u>tasks</u> in TRIPOS is in terms of messages. Message passing is done by switching pointers, rather than by copying, and in consequence the system is highly efficient. Each task has a single message or <u>work queue</u> and messages sent to a task are appended to the end of the queue. The system has a message sending primitive called 'qpkt' and a message receiving primitive called 'taskwait' which will block a task until there is a message available for it. Other primitives allow tasks to be halted and released, and the relative priority of tasks to be changed.

The filing system is implemented as a task running under the aegis of the kernel. It has a simple hierarchical directory structure with very elementary protection facilities. There is no notion of a user in the filing system: it is assumed that each user will have his own personal disc. The filing system is designed to be resilient against accidental corruption and easy to reconstruct if a disaster does occur. There are operations for loading programs down from the disc into memory so that they may be executed and for word or block level access to data files.

A standard part of the TRIPOS system is a debugging task which is invoked whenever there is a fatal error. This debugging program has the usual set of operations for inspecting registers and memory. Additionally, there are commands to control tasks and produce procedure call traces and tables of variables.

It was evident that TRIPOS would make a useful personal computer operating system for machines in the Processor Bank; however, a number of changes had to be made to the system where the Processor Bank model of a personal computer was inappropriate to the TRIPOS view. The most significant differences are that a processing server has no local discs and no directly attached terminal.

There is a single TRIPOS filing system held on the File Server shared by all of the versions of the system running in the Processor Bank. This required a complete rewrite of the TRIPOS filing system so that it could be mapped onto the files and indices provided by the File Server. As an interim measure, a very simple TRIPOS filing system was written which used the File Server as a remote virtual disc. For each machine in the Processor Bank, a file was set up to be the virtual disc for that machine's filing system. The filing system of one machine was deemed to be the master copy and this master machine was left running TRIPOS all of the time. The TRIPOS operating system allows two instances of the filing system on different devices to be online simultaneously. When a user acquired a processing server, the master filing system would be available in read-only mode to all processing servers, but could only be written into by the machine in charge of it. Thus, apart from the master, all other machines wrote into their own filing system rather than the master one. At the end of a session it was necessary to copy any important files back to the master filing system using a standard inter-filing system transfer program. This very rudimentary system was an illustration of how the File Server can be used in a low-level manner. The alterations needed in the TRIPOS system to make use of the File Server, instead of a local disc, were straightforward.

However, the implementation of a shared filing system to replace the interim one was a considerable task because of the synchronisation required in order to prevent updates being lost if two users accessed the same directory simultaneously. The necessary interlocking was obtained by use of the File Server facilities for supporting exclusive access to files. The way in which the TRIPOS filing system is organised is described in Section 4.5.

It was expected that moving the filing system onto the File Server might have lead to a reduction in the amount of code in the TRIPOS operating system, but this was not the case. The code required to map filing system operations into File Server transactions together with the extra work to be done to maintain interlocks and deal with clashes outweighs that required to deal with space allocation and disc driving in a stand-alone TRIPOS. However, one side effect of the use of the File Server is that the likelihood of data being corrupted by accident is greatly reduced and a less redundant, more efficient file representation can be used.

Since all machines running TRIPOS share the same filing system it is necessary to introduce the notion of a user so that there should be some degree of protection. When a TRIPOS system is loaded into a processing server, it first of all asks the user to identify himself using the standard Ring authentication machinery. If the user cannot prove his identity by quoting the correct password, the TRIPOS system will not allow him access to the filing system. If the check is successful, the user is allowed to continue and the system will make his home directory the current one. The way in which TRIPOS uses the Ring authentication system will be described more fully in Chapter Nine. This code too represents a further overhead beyond the requirements of an ordinary TRIPOS system.

Remote terminal access required the writing of a byte stream protocol package to support the virtual terminal protocol. The line editing functions of the stand-alone terminal TRIPOS system are done by the

Terminal Concentrator, although the internal TRIPOS terminal handler intercepts certain control codes that are used to switch input between tasks and signal interrupts.

The remaining respect in which TRIPOS required change was to deal with the way in which the Resource Manager connects terminals to loaded systems and controls time limits on sessions. TRIPOS is required to poll the Resource Manager at regular intervals or the processing server will be assumed to have crashed and it will be reclaimed (see Section 8.1). When a user quits from a TRIPOS session, the system will send a message to the Resource Manager to indicate that the processing server is no longer in use.

All of these changes were made in such a way that compatibility with the stand-alone TRIPOS system was preserved to the maximum extent. Only programs such as disc repairing utilities that relied on existence of a local disc and those programs that used the local terminal directly, rather than through the terminal handler, were lost. A consequence of the modifications is that the TRIPOS system now contains code to implement most of the Ring protocols and invoke many standard services so that it is very easy to bring up a new application under the TRIPOS system. The main penalty has been the increase in the size of the system. Another point is that much more of the system, in particular the Ring driving code, must remain intact after a software crash for the debugging program to work. However, the next chapter will show how the Processor Bank management system can be used to support remote debugging, thereby reducing the need for a substantial debugging program in the server itself.

7.8 The TRIPOS Filing Machine

An alternative approach to the provision of filing system facilities has been developed with the dual goals of avoiding some of the space penalties mentioned above, and of reducing the load imposed on the File Server by a number of processing servers running TRIPOS simultaneously. While this scheme is still at the experimental stage, it is worth describing here as an example of the use of processing servers and the File Server.

A particular processing server is dedicated to supporting the TRIPOS filing system and is known as the **TRIPOS Filing Machine.** This machine is loaded using the normal Processor Bank mechanisms and remains allocated continuously thereafter. It contains the only copy of the full TRIPOS filing system programs. In ordinary user's TRIPOS systems, the filing system code is replaced by a series of stubs which translate calls on the filing system into single shot protocol transactions with the Filing Machine. These include calls to open and close files as well as reading and writing data. The effect of this is to reduce by about one third the amount of memory taken up by the TRIPOS operating system in each user's machine. With eight or nine user machines running TRIPOS, the observed performance using the Filing Machine is superior to that obtained by their direct use of the File Server.

There are three main aspects of the Filing Machine. First there are the protocols used between the Filing Machine and its clients. They are made adequately reliable by a combination of idempotent definition of function and serial identification of successive calls. Where the response to a call is of a known and small size, the Filing Machine remembers the response until another call is received belonging to the same series. Thus, if a call is repeated the response can be re-issued directly. In cases where the response is not of a small predictable size, the operation involved is designed to be repeatable.

A client may have several series of calls in progress at one time and all requests are labelled with the series to which they belong. Writing to the File Server is done asynchronously – the Filing Machine's reply to a write request indicates that the material to be written is in the Filing Machine's memory, not that it has reached the File Server. Two variants of writing are supported, analogous to the single shot and full write of the File Server. The only significant difference is in an additional response to requests for writing large amounts of data. The Filing Machine may reply "Write already done" in addition to the normal "Go ahead on port P". This will occur when a client is attempting to repeat a write that has already been done; presumably because the final response went astray.

The second aspect of the Filing Machine is its relationship to the File Server. It is a perfectly ordinary client of the File Server, but it arranges to lessen the load imposed on the File Server in several ways. First it reads material in larger sized units than an ordinary TRIPOS would. This causes more useful data to be moved with the File Server's overheads only being incurred once. Secondly, the Filing Machine maintains a cache of recently accessed material, which has the effect of avoiding File Server reference completely for many of the system files in common use. Thirdly, the Filing Machine handles locking itself; the File Server's locking facilities are only used for protecting certain operations on directories so that the Filing Machine can coexist peacefully with the standard TRIPOS system.

Finally, in order to reduce the use made of the File Server to hunt through a hierarchical directory structure, the Filing Machine caches an abstract of those parts of the directory hierarchy it has had occasion to visit. The abstract is only a summary of the information in the directories and takes up less space than would be necessary to cache the directory blocks. Thus, when following a multi-level file title, it is usually unnecessary to read material from the File Server to verify the intermediate directories.

The success of the Filing Machine illustrates the value of not having to minimise the amount of communication that occurs over a high-speed network. The cost of sending some data around the Ring more than once is completely outweighed by the benefits of larger scale File Server operations and a caching system that knows what it is caching and why.

Processor Bank Management

8.1 The Resource Manager: functional description

The **Resource Manager** is the service that is responsible for controlling the allocation of processing servers from the **Processor Bank.** There are many issues of management associated with the allocation of computing resources; for example, should a certain class of users have priority at particular times of the day? Who can use which machines and so forth? These problems are common to both conventional time-sharing systems and the Processor Bank. The Resource Manager provides an effective range of management <u>mechanisms</u> capable of supporting whatever <u>policies</u> are used to settle questions of priority and privilege.

The Resource Manager has to maintain an allocation table recording which machines are allocated and for how long. Against the entry for each machine is a list of <u>attributes</u> describing the machine. The attributes are used to decide how best to satisfy the needs of a particular user. Attributes divide into two classes: generic machine types such as 'LSI4' and sub-attributes such as 'LSI4/10' - a slow processor - and 'LSI4/30' - a fast processor. The request made by a client for an allocation includes the attributes required of the allocated machine, the identity of the software to be loaded and a total allocation time limit. The Resource Manager consults its tables of users' privileges to see if the client is entitled to make such a request and if so, goes on to see if a suitable machine can be found. There is scope for endless ingenuity in the allocation strategy so that machines with scarce attributes will only be given away if no other machine will do. At present the following simple algorithm is employed: initially the tables are searched to see if there is a free machine with exactly the attributes required by the client and, if so, it is allocated. Otherwise, a second scan is conducted to find the machine with the least, or least valuable superfluous attributes. This is done by assigning a numerical weight to each attribute and choosing the machine with the least weight. The purpose of the algorithm is to cherish machines with valuable attributes since they are likely to be a scarce resource.

The Resource Manager instructs the **Ancilla** corresponding to an allocated machine to load a memory image into it. The loading file may be specified either as a File Server PUID or as a text name to be looked up in the Ancilla's filing system (see Section 7.6). When a client presents the Resource Manager with a loading request, the name of the memory image is passed over as a text string and the Resource Manager in turn hands the string on to the Ancilla.

There is an alternative form of loading request for accessing certain commonly used systems, for example the TRIPOS operating system. In this case the client passes over a string such as 'TRIPOS' which is recognised by the Resource Manager. For each system known to it, the Resource Manager has a table of configurations where each configuration specifies a loading file and set of attributes. When presented with a request for one of the built-in systems, the Resource Manager searches its allocation tables, trying each configuration of the system in turn, until one is found for which there is a suitable machine free. Thus suppose, as an example, that the Processor Bank contains machines of types 'A' and 'B', both of which support the TRIPOS portable operating system. If a client just asks for 'TRIPOS', a version running on either an A machine or a B machine will do, but the loading files obviously differ in each case. In the configuration table for TRIPOS there will be two entries: one against the 'A' attribute giving the name of the loading file for A machines and another with a different name for B machines. In addition to giving the name of the system, the client may specify a series of attributes which are merged with those in the configuration tables. Thus asking for 'TRIPOS' with the attribute 'BIGMEMORY' will obtain a version of TRIPOS in any machine with the big memory attribute, whereas asking with the attribute 'LSI4' would limit the machine to being one of the LSI4 family.

The Resource Manager is responsible for ensuring that one user may not interfere with machines belonging to another, that is to say it is concerned with issues of authentication. The current implementation of the Resource Manager has very rudimentary protection facilities in that it restricts control over a machine to the machine on behalf of which the allocation was made. In the case of allocations made via the **Session Manager** - the terminal user interface to the Resource Manager - control commands are only accepted from the terminal at which the original allocation request was made. Future versions of the Resource Manager will make use of the Ring user authentication system to be described in Chapter Nine. This will mean that control commands can be given from any terminal or machine, provided that the authority to give the command is demonstrated.

When a machine is allocated on behalf of another machine, rather than a user at a terminal, the allocated machine will quite often need to get in contact with the client machine. The machine may also wish to know how much time it has been given. Both of these needs are catered for by a Resource Manager information function. When an allocation request is made, a few bytes of data may be deposited with the Resource Manager. When the allocated machine calls the information function, these data bytes are included in the reply, together with details of the amount of time left in the allocation period. The most common use of the data bytes is to hold an address by which the allocated machine can get in contact with the owning machine.

The use of the information function should be contrasted with an alternative scheme whereby the data would be loaded into the memory of the allocated machine at some conventional position when the machine was started up. However, to provide the data that way is against the principle that processing servers are to be considered as personal computers without any restriction. Furthermore, there are problems with loading programs written outside the project (such as manufacturer's test programs) if certain areas of memory are prohibited to user code.

There are three ways in which an allocation can be terminated. One is by simply running out of time. Alternatively, an allocated machine may send a message to the Resource Manager to indicate that it has finished and the machine can be reclaimed. A similar function can be exercised by the owner of a machine instructing the Resource Manager to cancel the allocation. In all of these cases, the Resource Manager will arrange for the Ancilla to stop the processing server from executing. This is particularly important if the machine is, for example, regularly polling the File Server to maintain an interlock. Clearly this activity should be suppressed when the machine is no longer in use, otherwise supposedly idle machines will tie down system resources unnecessarily.

The Resource Manager provides an operation which allows a processing server to be reloaded, provided that the allocation period has not expired. This operation is normally used to run a fresh version of an operating system in the same machine if the system is accidentally corrupted or broken.

This reloading operation is only useful if there is a person present to observe the system crash. However, if an allocation is made on behalf of another machine, or if a user leaves his machine running unattended a crash would not be noticed and there is a potential for the machine remaining unproductive until the time allocation expires. To deal with this the concept of a short timer was introduced. When a machine is allocated, the client has to specify a short time interval, in addition to the total duration of the session. The Resource Manager expects the allocated machine to send a message at regular intervals to reset a time-out counter which is initially set to the short time interval. If the allocated machine fails to reset the counter in time, the Resource Manager will consider the machine to have crashed and reclaims it. For programs that are known to run for fixed, short periods the interval can be set larger than the total allocation period so that the program need not be concerned with the short timer.

In practical implementations, machines reset the short timer more frequently than is strictly necessary. This means that if a message is occasionally lost because of communication failures, or if the message is delayed because of congestion in either the processing server or the Resource Manager, no harm will be done. In consequence, the machine does not have to go to great lengths to get every message through, nor is the Resource Manager obliged to ensure that the reply gets back every time. This is another typical example of a tradeoff between lightweight protocols and (by implication) simple programs against greater use of communications bandwidth.

The Resource Manager provides some simple functions to support maintenance of processing servers. A suitably privileged user can cause a machine to be withdrawn from the Processor Bank, after the current owner has done with it. This command is used to prevent machines due for repair or maintenance from being allocated. There is a corresponding function to put a machine back into service after it has been withdrawn. The privileged user can ask the Resource Manager to load programs into a withdrawn machine so that test programs may be run. The Resource Manager will pass the request on to the Ancilla in the usual way.

8.2 The Resource Manager: implementation

The Resource Manager runs on a Z80-based small server. Requests are sent to it in the form of single shot protocol requests. The following functions are provided:

Information. This is the function used by a processing server to find out why it has been allocated and for how long. Exercising this function has the side effect of resetting the short timer to a value given in the request.

The reply gives information about the total allocation time left, the Ring station number of the machine owning the processing server and the data left with the Resource Manager by that machine (see the command function below). In addition there is information given about any outstanding terminal connection waiting with the Session Manager (see Section 8.4).

The owner of a processing server may reset the short timer rather than the server itself. This is so that a remote debugging program can reset the timer if it has stopped a processing server from executing instructions. The name of the machine for which information is sought is passed over as a string. A null machine name is interpreted as meaning the calling machine itself.

Finish. This command is used by a processing server to return itself voluntarily to the pool of free machines before the overall time limit has expired.

Command. This function is used to transmit commands to the Resource Manager. Commands are represented as textual strings. An allocation command (SYSNAME or SYSDESC below) is accompanied by six bytes of data which will be remembered by the Resource Manager and passed over when the information function is exercised in the way described above. Examples of possible commands are as follows:

SYSNAME name time-limit MCATTR attributes

This command causes a configuration of the named system, suitable for running on a machine with the requested attributes to be allocated and loaded, and to remain allocated for the time limit. The initial setting of the short timer is implicit because it is held in the table of configurations.

SYSDESC file time-limit initial-time-limit
MCATTR attributes

This command is used to load particular files in the Ancilla's filing system. The limit and attributes are treated in the same way as for the SYSNAME command. The initial time limit specifies the period within which the allocated machine must reset the short timer for the first time. If the program does not use the timer, this limit may be set to exceed the time limit.

SYSNAME name time-limit MCNAME machine

SYSDESC file time-limit initial-time-limit
MCNAME machine

These commands are used to reload an allocated machine. They are only available to the owner of the machine in question. The effect of the command is similar to the earlier examples of SYSNAME and SYSDESC commands.

RELEASE machine

The named machine, which must be owned by the client making the request, is returned to the pool of free machines. If a machine name is not given, all of the machines owned by the client are released.

WITHDRAW machine
DEPOSIT machine

These commands are intended for use by engineers when repairing machines in the Processor Bank. The WITHDRAW command takes a machine out of service and the DEPOSIT command replaces it. It is possible for engineers to use SYSNAME and SYSDESC commands to load test programs into withdrawn processing servers.

It is important that the Resource Manager should preserve the table of machine allocations, even if the software crashes. This is done by regularly copying the contents of the allocation table out to the File Server so that an up-to-date record will be kept in stable storage. Whenever the Resource Manager is reloaded, it reads down the table from the File Server so that any current allocations will persist. As well as the dynamic information about processing server allocations, the tables of machines and attributes are also kept on the File Server. This is so that a program can be run on a convenient machine in order to update this table when new machines are added to the Processor Bank or when a machine's attributes are to be modified.

8.3 The Resource Manager: extensions

An important feature of the way the Processor Bank is used in the Cambridge Distributed Computing System is that the client has complete and exclusive control over his machine for as long as he has booked it. There is no sharing of machines and if a user claims a machine for many hours and leaves it essentially idle the system takes no action. This is because, in our view, processing servers should be treated as personal computers once they have been allocated to a client. Clearly there should be rules to prevent valuable machines being retained for long periods and also to stop one user monopolising many machines simultaneously.

There is one respect in which the allocation of a machine for a continuous period is not reasonable. There are some computations which can be speeded up by spreading them over a number of machines so that the work is shared out. A classical example would be a program tracing some sort of decision tree where parallel branches of the tree may be pursued independently. Many such programs have the property that they can extended to a considerable degree of concurrency, yet at the same time, provided that one coordinating machine keeps running, the computation can recover from the loss of any other machine. It could be imagined that the user wanting to run such a program would ask for an allocation of machines until they are needed by someone else. At times when the Processor Bank is under-utilised, the computation will absorb many machines and as demand for processing servers by other clients builds up, the distributed computation will retreat back into a smaller set of machines. There is no reason why such a facility should not be provided by the Resource Manager, although to do so would increase the complexity of the allocation control policies because of the need to deal equitably with several such programs running at once.

Another feature which could be provided would be to arrange that, when an allocation period comes to an end, it is possible to try and renegotiate an extension to the time allowed on the machine. However, if this was relied upon to cause a sufficient turnover of machines to keep up with the demand for machines, it would be indicative of overloading in the Processor Bank and the need for more processing servers to be made available.

The Resource Manager is the obvious point at which to provide debugging facilities for processing servers. It was explained in Section 7.7 how the stand-alone TRIPOS system has a debugger that can be called down from disc into a crashed machine to conduct a post mortem examination. A similar function can be provided through the Resource Manager using the commands for reloading machines.

An alternative approach to debugging is to run a processing server under the control of a remote debugging program. The remote debugger can be provided in one of two ways: either as a program to be run in another processing server by the client, or as a standard shared service to which the client can connect a terminal. In the present system, a very simple remote debugger to be run on another processing server is available, but the extensions to the Resource Manager required to support it fully have yet to be written. The owner of the machine to be debugged will have to instruct the Resource Manager to enable the debugging machine to take control. This information will be passed on to the Ancilla which, in turn, will make the Ring interface of the machine accept debugging commands from the debugger. When the machine is returned to the Processor Bank, the Resource Manager will instruct the Ancilla to cancel the debugging session.

The short timer mechanism can be used to provide an automatic dumping service for processing servers that are left running unattended. If an allocated machine fails to honour the timer, the Resource Manager could be made to instruct the Ancilla to make a copy of the contents of the machine's memory and put it in the Ancilla's filing system from which it could be removed later on and inspected. This service might also be of use for a machine which is under the control of a person because, unlike the previous suggestion of loading a debugging program on top of a crashed machine, it would be possible to dump memory and then have the entire machine available for a debugging program that worked on the dumped memory image.

8.4 The Session Manager

The job of the Session Manager is to provide a mechanism for connecting remote terminals to systems loaded by the Resource Manager and also to provide users at remote terminals with a simple interface to the Resource Manager. For a user with a personal computer, rather than just a terminal, the Session Manager is redundant because all of its operations can be carried out by his own machine. Terminals are connected to the Session Manager using the virtual terminal protocol (see Section 6.6). Lines of input are converted to strings and sent to the Resource Manager as messages in the single shot protocol. The

Session Manager interprets the reply from the Resource Manager and displays an appropriate message upon the terminal. The Session Manager has some commands of its own, in addition to those passed to the Resource Manager. For example, the LIST command produces a table summarising the status of the machines in the Processor Bank, whether they are allocated or not, how long for and their owners. This information is derived from a series of calls to the Resource Manager to inspect its internal tables.

When a machine is allocated through the Session Manager, the terminal byte stream is made available to the newly allocated machine so the stream which was opened to the Session Manager then becomes the stream connecting the user's terminal to the program running in the allocated machine. This is arranged as follows: when the Session Manager makes up an allocation command for transmission to the Resource Manager, it includes the name of a connection service which can be looked up in the Name Server and will turn out to be a route back to the Session Manager. For a machine allocated through the Session Manager, the _information_ function provided by the Resource Manager will yield the name of the connection service and also indicate that there is a terminal stream pending connection. The processing server will then open a byte stream to the connection service. This event is recognised by the Session Manager which then uses the byte stream protocol _replug_ operation[1] to merge this new byte stream from the processing server with the one from the user's terminal.

It should be noted that this terminal connection scheme has to use the byte stream _replug_ operation because the Terminal Concentrators only support

----

[1] The _replug_ operation requires two byte streams to be open to a single machine. The effect is that the machines at the other ends of each of the byte streams are told of each other's addresses and instructed to use the other's address from then on. This leaves the two end machines in direct communication and at the same time disconnects the middle machine from both byte streams.

forwards connection from a virtual terminal to a host. The protocol does not allow a host to open a connection to a terminal. It would be possible to modify the protocol so that terminal connections were made by sending a request to the host which then opens a stream to the Terminal Concentrator. This would complicate the protocol however, and is unnecessary for organising connection to other computers, such as the University Computing Service where forwards connection is entirely adequate.

The Session Manager is not a privileged service; any user can write a command program that talks to the Resource Manager directly, using the single shot protocol. In the first implementation of the Resource Manager and Session Manager, they both ran in the same machine, communicating through an internal interface. More recently, the two have been split to free more memory space for the Resource Manager's use. The interface between them is public and in consequence users with personal computers can organise terminal connection to a processing server without the assistance of the Session Manager.

8.5 Examples of use

File Server garbage collector. The File Server's asynchronous garbage collector, designed to run on a processing server in parallel with normal operation of the File Server, is described in Section 4.4. When a garbage collection is required, the File Server sends a single shot request to the Resource Manager with a SYSDESC command specifying the File Server PUID of the memory image of the garbage collector. At the end of its run, the garbage collector signals to the Resource Manager that the machine can be freed. It should be noted that the garbage collector program is named by its PUID, rather than by a file title in the Ancilla's filing system. This is because the garbage collector is a highly privileged program and it is kept out of any, ordinary user accessible, filing systems in the interests of File Server integrity.

Pointing Machine Server. The Pointing Machine Server (see Section 6.7) requires a processing server to run the program that scans a wiring schedule and issues commands to the pointing machine. When a new operator logs onto the terminal connected to the Pointing Machine Server, it sends off a request containing a SYSDESC command. In this case the memory image is specified by an Ancilla filing system name because the software is less privileged and it is more convenient for it to be accessed by name so that new versions can be installed without having to update the program in the Pointing Machine Server.

TRIPOS. To obtain this system the user at a terminal engages in a dialogue as follows (user responses are shown in **bold** type):

Monitor> — this is the prompt produced by the control program in the Terminal Concentrator.

Monitor>**C SM** — the user attempts to open a terminal connection to the Session Manager.

*** 1 allocated — the Terminal Concentrator acknowledges the C command and opens a byte stream.

SM> — this is the prompt from the command line interpreter in the Session Manager.

SM>**SYSNAME TRIPOS 60 MCATTR LSI4**

the user requests that a machine with at least the attribute 'LSI4' be allocated to run a configuration of the TRIPOS operating system for up to sixty minutes.

Alpha allocated — the Resource Manager has found and loaded a suitable machine (called Alpha).

*** 1 RESET — this is the Terminal Concentrator reporting the byte stream replug operation.

TRIPOS starting

User: this is the TRIPOS operating system prompt inviting the user to login.

If the user wants to run a system of his own that has not been built into the Resource Manager, he will use a SYSDESC command instead of a SYSNAME command.

As an optimisation, the Session Manager provides a number of services that connect directly to particular systems without the user typing further commands. For example, if the user had said "C TRIPOS" rather than "C SM", the Terminal Concentrator would connect to the Session Manager, but with a different function code. This Session Manager service obeys an implicit "SYSNAME TRIPOS" command and if a suitable machine is free, the allocation and terminal connection are made as before.

The user may leave TRIPOS in a number of ways: if he obeys the FINISH command in the operating system or disconnects his terminal byte stream, the TRIPOS system will send a message to the Resource Manager to indicate that the machine is free. Alternatively, the user can open another terminal stream to the Session Manager and use the RELEASE command.

9 Protection and Authorisation

9.1 Protection in local area networks

Protection in local area networks is concerned with controlling access to services in accordance with policies decided externally. Services are called upon by message using the network, and it is for the code providing a particular service to implement policies about access. There must be information associated with the message on the basis of which decisions about protection may be made. This information may include, but not exclusively, the address of the machine from which the request is made and the identity of the principal[1] making the request. It is accordingly important to have methods of authentication of principals which shall be readily accessible and usable without great overhead by services in general.

In deciding whether or not a particular request should be honoured, there are various alternatives. Either the server itself may keep records of who is authorised to do what, or it may expect to be given some sign of authority which may be checked with an external agency. What is inevitable is that the onus is on the server to take the necessary decision. This is a consequence of the open nature of the system, in which there is no constraint at all placed on the use made of the Ring by the various machines attached to it. One could imagine a very different system in which messages were controlled at source; a machine would

---

[1] A principal is the term used to describe a name that may appear in an access control list. Usually a principal will stand for a particular user or program.

not be permitted to send a message requesting a service unless this was certified to be a proper action. Control in such a system would lie in the communication interfaces of the computers connected, which would form part of the protection envelope of the system as a whole. In a system like the present one, it is for servers to defend themselves against abuse by refusing to act except on the basis of proper requests.

Since the *bona fides* of a request must usually be determined by external reference, there is a subtle distinction between the implementation of protection in distributed and in centralised systems. Protection in centralised systems may be enforced much more strongly. For example, a call on a procedure to check credentials may simply not return if the credentials are bad. In a distributed system, all that can be done is to give advice on the prudence or otherwise of proceeding with the requested work.

In the development of the Cambridge Distributed Computing System the emphasis has been on devising a general mechanism for the expression of permission and authenticity. If the work is successful then we should see the same mechanism being used for checking purposes all over the system, because it should appear to be the most convenient way of doing the job (rather than as the result of an administrative *fiat*).

Whenever approaches to protection are discussed, it is necessary to be clear about the ground rules being applied. No attempt has been made to cater for interference with the Ring itself, by wiretapping or otherwise. If one were concerned about such interference, it would be necessary to make extensive use of encryption, for example in the manner proposed by Needham and Schroeder[2]. As a special case of this, we assume that machines on the Ring are properly authenticated by address: nobody maliciously alters the coding plugs in the stations.

----

[2] R.M. Needham & M.D. Schroeder. December 1978. 993-9. 'Security and Authentication in Large Networks of Computers'. *New York*: *Communications of the Association for Computing Machinery*, 21(12).

We also assume that another particular type of protection hazard is not important. It is possible to deny service of a particular type to others by bombarding the machine that provides the service in question with unsatisfiable requests. Although the service protects itself from abuse of the real resources it manages by checking authorisation, it may happen that so many of the machine cycles are taken up in rejecting bad enquiries that there is nothing left to handle good ones. This may apparently only be dealt with by the provision, at a very low level, of a rejection list, such that transmissions from a station, say A, to a station B that has A on its rejection list will be rendered abortive before any of B's cycles have been used. There is no such provision in the present system.

We are however concerned with transience of authorisation, and with the possibility of revocation of authority. The general approach taken depends upon the use of identifiers drawn from a very sparsely occupied space, these identifiers being passed for use as capabilities. To make use of a capability it is necessary to check it against a registry in which it will, if valid, be found. There is an important contrast here with the generally analogous use of capabilities in internal protection of computer memories. In the latter case it is possible to protect the capabilities themselves by hardware, keeping them physically separate from data and preventing any data operations from being performed on them. It is thus possible to interpret capabilities directly, without checking them for validity. In a distributed system there is no analogue of this state of affairs.

The use of capabilities should be distinguished carefully from the use of passwords and other secrets for authentication. Capabilities are issued as a result of authentication with the intention that they will pass from hand to hand for use as required. This is quite different from the treatment of passwords which are passed around as little as possible. Even so, care should be taken not to reveal capabilities unwisely.

9.2 The Active Name Table

The protection system used in the Cambridge Distributed Computing System is based upon the use of capabilities known as *keys*. Keys may be offered as proof of identity or privilege when requesting a service. The allocation of keys lies in the hands of the **Active Name Server.** This server maintains a table, called the **Active Name Table** (ANT) of all current keys and can tell a service whether or not a key offered by a client is valid. Thus keys are purely transitory in nature; for example the key identifying a user is only kept in existence for as long as the user remains logged in. Every time the user leaves the system his key is destroyed and when he returns to the system subsequently he must identify himself once more, by use of a password, in order to be issued with a key for use in the new session.

When a key is passed by a client to a server, the service will want to know who the key is for in most cases. To this purpose, a system wide naming scheme has been set up. Every protected entity (only users will be considered in the present discussion) is given a *name* which is an all time unique identifier drawn from a sparsely occupied space. There are various naming services on the Ring which will translate mnemonic names, such as user identifiers, into the corresponding name and *vice versa*. Names are public knowledge and do not indicate any aspect of privilege that they describe. Thus when protection is required, a name has to be accompanied by a suitable key. The operations supported by the Active Name Server are best described by considering the contents of the active name table as various operations take place. The table may be thought of as four columns, with a typical entry shown below:

1	2	3	4
MVW	A	CL	B

The significance of the columns is as follows[3]:

1 a name, in this case the user MVW
2 an access key A
3 the authority which created the access key for the user (Computer Laboratory)
4 a control key B

Suppose the user MVW wants to call a service requires proof of his identity and association with the Computer Laboratory. He has to supply the service with his name, MVW, and the access key A. The service may then approach the Active Name Server to enquire if there is an entry in the table with the values <MVW, A, CL> in its first three columns. In this example there is and the service is assured that the request has been sent either by MVW's computer, or one he has authorised to act on his behalf by telling it his access key.

There may be entries in the table for other users belonging to the same authority as MVW, and users belonging to other authorities. The table below has been augmented by another member of the Computer Laboratory called GSM and a student user called JR:

MVW	A	CL	B
GSM	P	CL	Q
JR	X	STU	Y

If the student, JR, attempts to use the service that is only available to members of the Computer Laboratory, the Active Name Server will report that there is not an entry in the table with the values <JR, X, CL> in the first three columns.

The purpose of the control key is to protect the entries in the table from unauthorised change. Any

---

[3] In the interests of clarity of presentation, different terms are used here to describe the protection system than those coined by its author. His terms for those used in the text are as follows: active name - active object; name - PUID; access key - TUID; control key - TPUID; authority - authentity.

request to alter, or remove an entry in the table must be accompanied by the control key. Thus, for example, if the user GSM wishes to remove his entry from the table he will instruct the Active Name Server to delete the entry with <GSM, CL, Q> in the first, third and fourth columns. Since the right to remove an entry from the table lies with the holder of the control key it is not possible for a machine that has been passed the access key alone to delete the corresponding entry. By using the control key to destroy entries in the table, it is possible to revoke a privilege that has been passed on.

Some users can act under a number of authorities and in consequence there may be a number of entries in the table for the same name. In the following example, the user MVW appears as a member of the Computer Laboratory and also with the powers of a professor:

```
MVW    A    CL    B
MVW    C    PRF   D
```

The two entries have distinct access keys, A and C. Thus when MVW calls any service he must decide which key is the correct one to pass. Sometimes this is inconvenient, particularly if there is a service which is only available to professors in the Computer Laboratory when both keys are required. The Active Name Server allows a single name and access key to appear several times over in the table thus:

```
MVW    A    CL    B
MVW    A    PRF   E
```

Each entry has a different control key so that MVW may selectively remove either of the two entries. When he calls the restricted service, he will pass over the pair <MVW, A> and the service will ask the Active Name Server to report if it can find entries matching both <MVW, A, CL> and <MVW, A, PRF> in the table.

It is also possible to have the same key against different names. Thus it could be arranged that all visitors to the Computer Laboratory are issued with the same access key every time they log in, as in the ANT entries shown below:

WDS	K	VIS	U
JGM	K	VIS	V

Clearly this would only be sensible if both WDS and JGM have identical powers, i.e. those of a visitor. Any service accepting a request from a visitor should be aware that the name that accompanies the access key is not guaranteed to be correct, although the service is safe to assume the request has come from a visitor. Thus for example, any charges for the service should be made against a general visitor's account, but the name can be used to direct printed output because there is no advantage in WDS pretending to be JGM in this respect. From the point of view of protection, JGM and WDS are pseudonyms.

The values in column three of the table indicate the authority conveyed by the rest of the entry and are set up when the entry is created. The authority is a name, much as MVW is the name of a user. When an entry in the table is to be created, the Active Name Server must be told the name for placing in column one and the name of the authority for placing in column three. The access and control keys are invented by the server and returned as the result of the operation. When an entry is made, the server must check that the agent responsible is entitled to use the authority. Authorities are recognised by the presence of a distinguished name 'AUT' in column three of their entries in the table. Thus in the example below S is an access key for use of the authority CL:

CL	S	AUT	T

The entry for MVW as a member of the Computer Laboratory would have been made by a service knowing the access key S. This service would have required him to prove his identity by quoting a password or by some other form of external validation. The request made by this service to the Active Name Server had the arguments (S, CL, MVW). First, the key S had to be checked by looking for an entry in the table with <CL, S, AUT> in the first three columns, and then the entry for MVW was made in the form below:

MVW   A   CL   B

The keys A and B were given back to the service making the entry. Obviously the access key, A, has to be given to MVW in order to be useful, but it is a matter of choice whether MVW is given B as well so that he may remove himself from the table.

The ability to create new authorities may be controlled by knowledge of the access key G from the following table entry:

AUT   G   AUT   H

In the previous illustrations, all of the examples have been framed in terms of human users. The operations of the ANT are much more general: they can be employed by programs to identify themselves and to protect a wide range of resources and privileges. In Chapter Five, the need to control who may alter the bootstrap files for small servers was discussed and in Chapter Eight, on Processor Bank management, the privilege of remote control over a processing server was introduced. Both of these are examples of the sort of protection which can be achieved through use of the ANT.

9.3 Implementation

The Active Name Server is currently a Z80-based small server and has room for over 500 entries in its table which is sufficient for the model system, but would need to be extended in a larger system. The ANT is kept entirely in memory so that access to it will be fast. To guard against failures in either the service software or the server hardware, the table is automatically copied out to the File Server so that entries will not be lost. The File Server PUID for the back up table is secret and only exists in the code of the Active Name Server, so that the information will remain secure.

All of the functions of the Active Name Server are implemented in terms of the single shot protocol. Entries in the ANT have an associated timeout which specifies how long the entry is to remain in the table. Thus, if breakdowns in communication cause spurious entries to be left in the table, they will decay continuously and eventually expire. The Active Name Server provides an operation which may be used to reset the timeout for a particular entry, provided that the call is accompanied by the control key for the entry. The Active Name Server uses the CLOCK service provided by the **Logger** in order to observe the passage of time and decide when to remove entries from the ANT.

Names and keys take the form of 64-bit values with 48 of the bits being chosen at random so that as capabilities they are difficult to forge. In addition, there is a field within them which indicates an ANT serial number. The serial number can be used to distinguish between keys issued by different Active Name Servers as might be the case if several of them are provided so that a larger table can be maintained. A server in receipt of a key can extract the field holding ANT serial number and use this to select the appropriate Active Name Server at which to check the key. Names and keys are made using a generally available service called 'NEWPUID' (names are also known as Permanent Unique Identifiers) that runs on the same machine as the Active Name Server. The NEWPUID service returns a 54 bit unique identifier comprising a 48 bit random number and an eight bit serial number identifying the random number generator used. In this case the serial number allows multiple versions of the NEWPUID service to run simultaneously without the risk of two of them generating exactly the same unique identifier.

When an ANT is set up, there is the problem of making the keys for the various authorities and distributing them. The Active Name Server recognises one machine with the name 'SOAP' (Source Of All Privilege) which is allowed to create entries in the ANT without offering an access key for an authority. This machine is thereby the root of all protection on the ring since it is responsible for generating the access keys required by the several authorities. SOAP has a table defining who may claim the right to exercise a particular authority. The table has three fields: the name of the client, an authority by which the client must be authenticated and the authority the client is entitled to control. A typical entry in the table is shown below

GSM USR PRF

This entry indicates that a client presenting an access key for the name GSM with the authority USR can be issued with access and control keys for the authority with the name PRF.

Summary of Active Name Server functions

verify [access key, name, authority] -> boolean

This is the verification function for an access key. The authority parameter is only the name of the authority. Thus authority can be checked by anyone.

check [access key, control key, name, authority] -> boolean

This function is similar to the **verify** operation with the addition of a check on the validity of the control key argument.

get key [name, authority, access key, timeout] -> access key, control key

This is the operation to generate a new entry in the table. The access key parameter must be an access key for the authority against which the new entry is to be made. The timeout parameter specifies in seconds how long the entry may remain in the ANT if it is not explicitly removed earlier.

enhance [access key, control key name, authority, authority access key, timeout] -> control key

This is the operation to make a further entry for an access key (the first parameter) in the ANT. There must be an entry present in the ANT for the name given by the third parameter with access and control keys given by the first and second parameters respectively. The fifth parameter must be an access key for the authority against which the new entry is to be made. The timeout parameter specifies how long the entry may remain in the ANT if it is not explicitly removed earlier.

refresh [access key, control key, name, authority, timeout]

This operation is used to reset the timeout associated with an entry in the ANT. If the timeout parameter is zero, the entry will be deleted from the table forthwith.

9.4 User authentication

One of the problems in a network offering several user orientated services is the frequency with which a user must reauthenticate himself as each different service is used. Using the Active Name Server it is possible to arrange that a user need only authenticate himself once to a central authentication service and obtain an access key which can be presented thereafter at every service. Thus, when negotiating with a service, a user can pass over his name and an authenticating access key so that the service will be assured of the authenticity of the client.

On the Ring there is a service called 'USERAUTH' which provides a user authentication facility. All operations are in terms of textual passwords of up to eight characters and are implemented using the single shot protocol. The simplest operation checks the correctness of a password for a given user name. To obtain an access key, the <u>authenticate</u> function is used. It takes the user's name, password and an initial timeout as arguments. If the password is correct, an access key will be created for the user name against the authentity 'ring user' and returned. The remaining operation supported by the user authentication service is one to change a password. This function requires the user's name and previous password to be quoted, and, together with the new one, to be put into the server's tables.

The user authentication system is used by the TRIPOS operating system when it is loaded into a processing server. Once the user's terminal stream is connected to the server (as described in Chapter Eight) the TRIPOS system asks the user for his user identifier (normally his initials). There is a table relating textual user identifiers to authentication system names. The system next prompts the user for his password. It is sent, together with the user's name, to the user authentication service for verification. Provided that the service is satisfied that the password is correct, an access key and control key will be returned to TRIPOS. The TRIPOS system will remember this information, together with the user's name and the authority under which he was logged on, and this data is referred to as the user's **UID set**. Once the TRIPOS system has accepted a user's identity, it will permit him to use the filing system, making his home directory current. The operating system will refresh the UID set at regular intervals so that it remains in the ANT. When the user finishes with TRIPOS, it deletes the entry in the ANT corresponding to the UID set. The advantages of using the Ring authentication system for TRIPOS are that it is not necessary for TRIPOS to keep a password file in its relatively insecure filing system and also that it is possible to open authenticated byte streams for file transfer and virtual terminal connection (see Section 9.5) without requoting passwords.

The basic user authentication system is extended to deal with the control of user's privileges, such as the ability to use certain machines, run restricted programs or consume valuable resources by introducing a service known as the **Privilege Manager**. Privileges are represented by entries in the ANT containing an authority called 'privilege'. The Privilege Manager expects the user to supply an access key for himself and an indication of the privilege by giving its name. If the Privilege Manager's tables show that the user is allowed the privilege, the Privilege Manager tells the Active Name Server to make a new entry in the ANT of the form

PRI X 'privilege' Y

Thus X is an access key for the privilege called 'PRI'. The client may ask that the access key X be a brand new key if it is desired to treat the privilege as an independent object. Alternatively, X may be an already existing access key if it is wanted to associate a set of privileges with the same key. In the present system, the ability to update the tables in SOAP, the User Authentication Server and the Privilege Manager, are all represented in terms of privileges. When, for example, the tables in SOAP are to be changed, SOAP is not concerned with who is making the alteration, but just that they are a holder of the appropriate privilege.

There are programs within the TRIPOS operating system for maintaining a collection of UID sets in existence so that a user may retain several privileges simultaneously. There are commands to edit the contents of the collection and to select which privileges are to be used when protected services are invoked.

It is proposed in the future to arrange that the Processor Bank management system described in Chapter Eight will take advantage of the user authentication mechanisms to control the privileges of being able to load and remotely debug processing servers. The present system does not do so because the Active Name Server was not fully developed at the time that the Resource Manager was implemented. When a machine is allocated, an entry will be made in the ANT particular to the allocation. Any subsequent request to the

Resource Manager to reload the machine, or so forth, will only be allowed if the access key from the ANT entry can be quoted. Thus, the loading and debugging operations provided by the Processor Bank management system can be treated as privileges within the protection system. A consequence of this is that the Resource Manager will be less of a privileged service and there can be a number of independent Resource Managers implementing different control policies for different parts of the Processor Bank. Each Resource Manager will only be able to load those machines for which it had a suitable access keys. Allocation periods would be enforced by virtue of the timeouts on ANT entries which would render the access keys for a machine useless once the allocation period had expired.

9.5 Authenticated byte streams

When a byte stream is opened, a name and access key pair may be optionally included in the open packet to authenticate the source of the byte stream. The most common use of authenticated byte streams is for file transfer using a protocol based on byte streams. A program called 'TAKEFILE' reads files from remote filing systems. If TAKEFILE is able to open a byte stream that can be verified as coming from an authenticated user of the machine containing the files, the latter will interpret the name of the file to transfer as being within that user's principal directory on the remote machine, otherwise a public directory will be used. Thus, a user's files may not be read remotely unless they are publicly accessible, other than by opening an authenticated byte stream. There is an analogous program called 'GIVEFILE' that can be used to copy a file to a remote filing system and it too makes use of authenticated byte streams in the same way.

Authenticated byte streams may also be used to open virtual terminal connections. If the host machine can verify the access key passed in the open block, there is no need for it to ask the user to give his password and authenticate himself. The host will have to translate the authentication system name (a 64-bit number) into the corresponding user identifier. This can be done by lookup in a table local to the host or alternatively by invoking a service called 'PS.MAP'. This service has a table of users and their various names on different systems. PS.MAP will translate a name in one name domain to its equivalent in another.

It would thus be appropriate for the terminal concentrator to conduct an initial user authentication negotiation with the user when he first uses a terminal and thereafter open authenticated byte streams as he connects terminal streams to machines so that he need not authenticate himself again. When the user leaves the terminal he should use a command to the concentrator in order to cancel the UID set it has been recording.

10 Review

This book has been concerned with the design and implementation of an experimental distributed computing system which is now in everyday use by members of the Computer Laboratory at Cambridge. In common with all experimental systems, work is continuing to make extensions, to improve it and to increase performance. The system has grown substantially over a period of time, with more than fifty devices attached to the Ring including more than fifteen machines in the Processor Bank. In this respect the experiment has grown beyond a small-scale trial into a practical system serving a large and demanding user community. The fact that the system has sustained this growth gives us confidence in the approach adopted at Cambridge and confirms the rectitude of many of the design decisions made during the course of the project. It would be hard to over emphasise how important practical experience is in the construction of large software systems. We hope that the description of the work at Cambridge will benefit others and stimulate the building of further systems in the exciting and innovative area of distributed computing.

Central to the Cambridge Distributed Computing System is the Processor Bank sustaining a collection of machines of various types. We have observed that users are quite selective in detail in their choice of machines. Frequently, the motivation is a reflection of the availability of particular software systems on the different machines and, of course, the performance of each type of machine at different sorts of computing has an effect. Without the centralised management of computing resources imposed by the Processor Bank model, the necessary flexibility to enable users to switch from one machine to another would not exist.

An important side-effect of the use of diverse machines has been the increase in the production of portable software so that programs can be supported on different machines. To a considerable degree this has followed from a conscious decision to use high-level languages wherever possible, and some effort has been taken to make the commonly used languages available over a wide spectrum of different computers. The considerable use of servers on the Ring to provide operating system services has enhanced the uniformity between systems. For example, nearly all machines use the Printer Server for the production of hardcopy output. As a general principle, all of the interfaces within the system have been exposed from the lowest level up. The entire collection of servers can be said to comprise an 'open' distributed system in the sense that users and operating systems can decide which facilities are useful to them and which are not. As an example, consider the Printer Server. Its interface is very low-level; it accepts a single byte stream at a time, representing a document as an ASCII character stream. If it is busy printing when a byte stream connection is attempted, the server simply refuses it; there is no attempt at spooling. For TRIPOS systems this imposes no difficulty; the user creates a task which runs the listing program and this task loops until it can gain access to the printer. Machines like CAP have spooling systems for output and here it is a simple matter for the despooling machinery to poll for use of the printer whenever there is output to print off. If, on the other hand, the interface to the Printer Server had been through a Ring-wide spooling system it is possible that CAP may not be able to blend its view of despooling with that of the central service. This remark does not reject a central spooling service - which would be of value to TRIPOS - but says that the low level interface to the printer itself should be public.

The services that go to make up the distributed operating system mainly run on small servers. These machines are inexpensive to make and have turned out to be very reliable in practice. Their failure rate is comparable to that of Ring stations and repeaters, and this can be directly attributed to the simplicity of their design. From the point of view of programming services, the provision of an individual machine in which software can be written without fear of interference with or from other programs using the same machine is an important factor. The small servers are a cost-effective approach by means of which to implement basic services in a distributed fashion. Hand in hand with the servers themselves go the Boot Server and the arrangements for loading, dumping and restarting servers. For much of the time the system runs without the attention of an operator, although failures and errors are reported so that in the event of difficulties an operator can deduce what is going on and take appropriate steps. This is a very important point because a distributed system, unlike a single machine, cannot be easily stopped to give the operator time to sort it out. In a distributed environment, errors frequently show up as congestion at a particular point leading to degraded performance rather than a total collapse.

Much of the uniformity of the system comes from the pervasiveness of the use of the Name Server throughout the system. It is built in at the lowest level and imposes a global pattern on the names of services and by extension to the names of programs to drive those services. For example, on all of the machines in the system, the file transfer program is called "GIVEFILE". In addition to static names, for example those of machines such as ALPHA and standard services such as DAT, we have observed the emergence of so-called 'dynamic' names where a name maps not onto the service directly but to an intermediary that causes the required service to be spawned when it is needed. One example of this is the way in which the name 'RATS-TRIPOS' is mapped onto the Session Manager so that when a user connects a terminal to 'TRIPOS' a processing server is allocated to him. This idea can be generalised and a host of dynamic service names built into the Resource Manager tables as required. In fact the present scheme does not deal with dynamic services perfectly, because a client will be aware of the difference in protocol when connecting via the Resource Manager and Session Manager as opposed to connecting directly to a static service. A topic of current research is to improve this by arranging that an intermediary can forward a connection request to a dynamically allocated server. The Resource Manager can be made responsible for control of the name of a dynamic service so that it can intercept connections to unavailable services, yet at the same time not have to handle connections to services that have been set up. Since the naming of dynamic services will be in the hands of the Resource Manager, the service names can be equated with the names of the corresponding loading files in the Ancilla's filing system, thereby avoiding the problems of control over names inherent in the present 'add name' and 'delete name' Name Server functions. The existence of a tidy mechanism for running dynamic services would also have the advantage of making it easier for operating systems to organise distributed computations in a coherent and uniform manner, so that user programs may reap the benefits of distributed computation.

One constraint on the utility of the Processor Bank is the time it takes to allocate and load a processing server. At present, this process takes a number of seconds and is comparable to the time taken to get logged in to many time-sharing systems. If the user intends to use the allocated machine for many minutes the overhead is not appreciable, but it does rule out the possibility of allocating a processing server for very short-term services such as finding out if someone has sent you mail over the network. There is scope for reducing the overall loading time by pre-loading free machines with popular systems and hierarchical loading so that, for example, machines could be pre-loaded with the TRIPOS operating system and only the application package called down on top of the operating system in response to a user's request. In the context of the grand design of the system rather than the model implementation the problem would not be so noticeable, since very simple operations would be the province of the user's small personal computer built into his terminal and processing servers would be used entirely for more intensive activities.

In the Cambridge Distributed System, by way of contrast with other systems, all permanent memory is concentrated in the File Server and individual machines do not have private, local discs. From the point of view of sharing data and this has enormous benefits. For example, all TRIPOS users, whatever variety of processing server they happen to use and whichever machine they happen to be allocated at any one time all coexist within the same filing system. The fact that the TRIPOS and CAP filing systems, which are quite different in philosophy, are both supported testifies to the success of the universal file server model. It is also relevant to note the use made of the File Server by several of the small servers to back up their data structures in permanent memory, so that it is preserved in the event of the server being restarted or moved. This mode of use depends greatly upon the simplicity of the protocol for transferring data and the use of unique identifier 64-bit strings to name material without recourse to complex directory structures. Given the sharing of data between machines, the presence of at least rudimentary interlocking has proved essential. A facility of the File Server that is not used heavily is that of the special file; in most systems, special files are used only to hold the data structures of filing system directories and it can be questioned whether or not a simpler mechanism could be devised.

Since the File Server occupies such a central position in the system, its performance is paramount. From experience with the TRIPOS Filing Machine, it can be suggested that to obtain the best from the File Server it should be used as a wholesaler of data rather than delivering data in penny packets. Certainly the

File Server should be implemented on a processor with sufficient power to support the loads made upon it, otherwise it will become a bottleneck. In particular, it must be able to accept requests even while it is engaged in a data transfer otherwise the impact of many machines pounding away trying to be heard will be adverse.

An innovative feature of the system is that authentication and protection mechanisms have been built in from the lowest level. It has been remarked that in a distributed system the protection mechanisms can only offer advice on the veracity and timeliness of a request from a client. Perhaps the most noticeable aspect of incorporating authentication into even the most basic protocols is that the user has only to identify himself once and thereafter software can pass around the necessary unique identifiers without any further user involvement. Thus, for example, when transferring files between filing systems the user does not have to quote his user identifier or password since this information is implicit in the unique identifiers passed in the course of setting up the transfer.

In the area of protocols, considerable advantage has been taken of the performance of the Cambridge Ring. All of the protocols are very simple and rely on the two facts that the Ring is inherently reliable and that the time taken to transmit data between machines is minimal compared to the time it takes the machines to process the data. As a particular example, the single shot protocol is very close to many message based inter-process communication systems and it has proved straightforward in practice to add Ring protocol software to existing operating systems. There has also been some speculation that very similar primitives to those of the Ring protocols can be used within a single machine for inter-process communication and that this could be extended to facilitate multi-machine computations using a uniform communication system.

A respect in which limitations can be perceived is that of processing server ring interfaces. As described earlier in the book, these are based on 8X300 microprocessor systems and provide packet protocol handling and remote control. This leaves higher level protocols, in particular the byte stream protocol which forms the foundation of the virtual terminal protocol in the hands of the processing server. It has been observed that using screen-based software driving unintelligent terminals imposes a heavy load on the processing server, especially when single character working is involved. There are a number of remedies to this deficiency. One is to build more intelligence into Terminal Concentrators and design a screen-based protocol in order to reduce the traffic between host and terminal. This also accords with the wider view of the system in which each user's terminal would include some local processing power and could support a higher level protocol. Recent changes in the availability of hardware make it possible to construct Ring interfaces of adequate performance using less restrictive machines than the 8X300 with more memory space so that byte stream handling could be incorporated into the interface, reducing the load on the processing server. This would also have an advantage when new types of machine are incorporated into the Processor Bank since less software would have to be written before the machine could communicate with other services.

To conclude, it has been our aim to describe the present state of the Cambridge Distributed System as an example of the application of local area network technology. In this new area of development it is too early to arrive at an objective statement about the best way to employ such technology to its greatest effect. The situation could be compared to that in the early days of time-sharing, whereas now in the light of experience obtained by the building of many different systems the field is well understood. It is our hope that others will feel encouraged to build practical systems and put them to the test and that they may benefit from our experience recorded here.

Appendix: Byte Stream Protocol Specification

M.A. Johnson[1]

1 Introduction

This document describes the byte stream protocol in use on the Cambridge Ring. The byte stream protocol is built on top of the packet protocol [Annex A]. It provides a pair of synchronised byte streams, and corrects all errors detected by the packet protocol. It is assumed that undetected errors will be sufficiently rare to be ignored, but there are facilities for resetting to a standard state if otherwise unrecoverable errors do happen. Acknowledgements are used to ensure data integrity, but there is no 'negative acknowledge'. It is intended that all erroneous packets be ignored, and that the timeout mechanisms of the byte stream protocol should repeat unacknowledged packets.

The acknowledgements also provide flow control, in order to ensure that a transmitter does not send more data than the recipient has committed himself to accepting. In order that the timeout mechanisms should not lead to futile communication during periods when there is no data to send or nowhere to put it, it is possible for either the transmitter or the recipient to stop the traffic (and assume responsibility for restarting it).

---

[1] This appendix is based upon a document called "Ring Byte Stream Protocol Specification" written by M.A. Johnson of the Computer Laboratory, University of Cambridge.

2 Scope

The main part of this document describes the byte stream protocol without reference to the setting up of connections. (The protocol generally used for initial connection is described in Annex B.) Additional restrictions, such as the maximum size of packet to be used, may also be agreed in advance, but any such agreement is not part of the definition of the byte stream protocol.

Subsets of this protocol could be regarded as a 'block stream protocol' or a 'packet stream protocol'. However, the only interface an implementation is obliged to provide is at the byte stream level. Any other interface is liable to cause confusion and is to be discouraged.

3 Commands

Each packet consists of:

1 A command referring to reception of data,
2 A command referring to transmission of data,
3 The data itself,

or alternatively consists of:

4 A control command referring to the transaction as a whole.

In order that repetitions of packets can be identified as such, commands are given sequence numbers. In this document, the sequence numbers are represented as subscripts on command names.

There are two possible commands for transmission. $DATA_n$ indicates that the packet contains data. $NODATA_n$ is sent instead when there is no data immediately available to send; it is used to prevent the recipient from timing out. A $NODATA_n$ will be followed by a $DATA_n$ when data eventually becomes available.

Similarly, there are two commands for reception. RDY_n indicates that packets with sequence number less than n have been successfully received, and that the recipient is now ready to receive packet n. $NOTRDY_n$ is sent when it is required to acknowledge the receipt of packets with sequence number less than n but the recipient is not yet ready for another packet. A RDY_n should be issued later when the recipient is able to receive the data.

The DATA and RDY commands are called **essential elements** of the protocol. They must be acknowledged within a certain time interval: otherwise they should be retransmitted. The sender of an essential element is responsible for retransmitting after a timeout. The NODATA and NOTRDY commands are called **non-essential elements** of the protocol. They act only as acknowledgements, and are not themselves acknowledged. The issuer of a non-essential element is responsible for issuing the corresponding essential element some time later (after an interval which will typically be longer than the timeout interval).

There is also a null command, which may be used when there is no requirement to send any particular command.

There are two control commands, which refer to the pair of byte streams taken together. The first is RESET, which is performed on request from higher level software, and may be generated from within the byte stream protocol under serious error conditions. If a RESET is generated internally, it must be reported to the user of the byte stream. A RESET command must be sent in both directions in order to ensure resynchronisation. When a RESET is sent, all received data should be ignored until a RESET is received in reply. If no RESET is received within a timeout interval, then it should be sent again. If an unexpected RESET is received, then a RESET should be sent in reply. After a RESET, the initial state (to be defined in detail later) should be entered, and the normal transactions resumed. It will usually be the case that one party has initiated the RESET and will deal with all the timeouts, but the symmetry of RESET ensures that it does not matter if both ends initiate RESETs simultaneously.

Any data awaiting transmission when a RESET occurs should be discarded, as should any data which has been received but not yet submitted to the user of the byte stream. The completion of a RESET must be notified to the user of the stream in such a manner that synchronisation can be recovered.

The second control command is CLOSE, which again is normally performed on request, but which may be internally generated under error conditions. It requests that the transaction be terminated immediately. The response to a CLOSE is a CLOSE. CLOSE may be repeated if not acknowledged within a timeout interval, but it must be borne in mind that the other process may have terminated itself and thus be unavailable to reply.

4 State transition diagram

The actions necessary to implement the protocol are expressed in a state transition diagram. The RESET and CLOSE functions are ignored, since they override everything else. Transmission and reception are symmetrical, and a single state transition diagram is presented for both on the following page. In a two way conversation, there will be four incarnations of the state table active at once. Some notes on the table follow:

There are three states.

E: An essential element ($DATA_n$ or RDY_n has been sent). An acknowledgement (RDY_{n+1} or $DATA_n$ respectively) is expected within the timeout interval.

N: A non-essential element ($NODATA_n$ or $NOTRDY_n$) has been sent. No response is required, although a retransmission may be required.

I: Idle state. A non-essential element ($NOTRDY_{n+1}$ or $NODATA_n$) has been received. Nothing further

State \ Event	E_{rep} $DATA_{n-1}/RDY_n$	E_{exp} $DATA_n/RDY_{n+1}$	N_{exp} $NODATA_n/NOTRDY_{n+1}$	Timeout	Buffer ready
E	Retransmit $RDY_n/DATA_n$ E	Empty/fill buffer n+: = 1 Buffer ready? yes: RDY_n $/DATA_n$ E no: $NOTRDY_n$ $/NODATA_n$ N	— I	Retransmit $RDY_n/DATA_n$ E	— E
N	Retransmit $NOTRDY_n/NODATA_n$ N	Protocol error	Protocol error	— N	Transmit $RDY_n/DATA_n$ E
I	Protocol error	Empty/fill buffer n+: = 1 Buffer ready? yes: RDY_n $/DATA_n$ E no: $NOTRDY_n$ $/NODATA_n$ N	— I	— I	— I

need be sent until the corresponding essential element (RDY_{n+1} or $DATA_n$) is received. However, it is legal to repeat the previous essential element. If the previous essential element was DATA, then the data itself need not be included in the packet. (For the motivation behind this rule, see the 'Idle handshake' section.)

There are five events.

E_{rep} An essential element which is a repetition of an earlier essential element. Since the original reception will have incremented the local sequence number, this will be RDY_n or $DATA_{n-1}$.

E_{exp} An essential element with the expected sequence number, i.e. RDY_{n+1} or $DATA_n$.

N_{exp} A non-essential element with the expected sequence number, i.e. $NOTRDY_{n+1}$ or $NODATA_n$.

Timeout
(waiting for response to essential element)

Buffer ready
(i.e. room for more data or more data to send)

Each box of the diagram gives the action to be taken ("-" means "do nothing") and, at the bottom, the state to be entered next. Valid state transitions are shown in the diagram below. Proceeding along the arrows marked "+" cause the local copy of the sequence number (n) to be incremented.

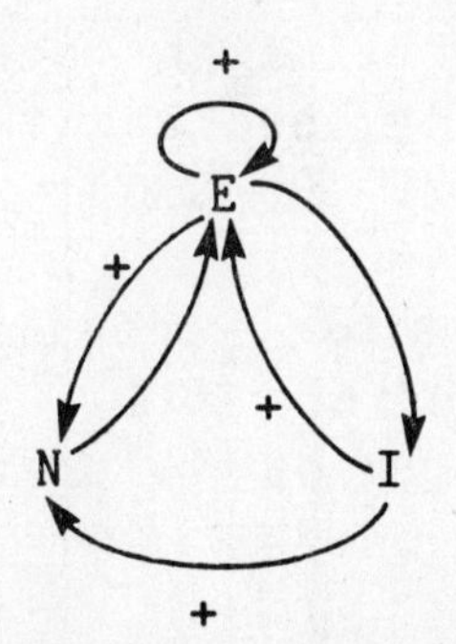

Initially, and after a RESET, the receivers should be in state N with sequence number 0, and the transmitters should be in state I with sequence number -1. As soon as a receiver has buffer space for the first packet (Buffer ready event), it will send RDY_0 and go to state E. The transmitter regards this as event E_{exp}, increments its sequence number to 0, and transmits either $DATA_0$ or $NODATA_0$.

Some boxes in the transition table are marked 'protocol error'. These states should not occur if both ends are implemented correctly and the packet protocol does not give undetected errors. Any other unexpected or uninterpretable packet is also a protocol error. The reaction to a protocol error may be implementation dependent - the erroneous packet may be ignored, or a RESET or CLOSE may be attempted.

5 Idle handshake

As described so far, the protocol does not include an idle handshake. Thus a failure at one end of a connection during an idle period will not be noticed at the other end until it restarts the traffic. For many applications this is undesirable.

A small modification to the state transition table enables this problem to be solved at little cost. In state 'I', a timer can be set, and if it expires, the previous essential element should be repeated. This puts the sender back into 'E' state, and the standard protocol mechanisms continue the transaction - which will usually terminate with an N_{exp} event and a consequent return to 'I' state. Note that the 'previous essential element' might have been 'DATA'. Since this data has already been acknowledged, it is defined to be legal to repeat the DATA command without including the actual data.

Note that an implementor provides the idle handshake for his own benefit. It is for this reason that it is an optional feature of the protocol.

6 Representation

This section defines the bit patterns used to represent the commands described above. A packet contains between 1 and 1024 'data minipackets' (i.e. not counting header, route and checksum). These are numbered from 0 upwards, in the order in which they are sent and referred to as 'words' below. Bits in a word are numbered from d0 (least significant) to d15 (most significant).

The layout of a packet is either:

```
  word 0: command referring to reception of data
  word 1: command referring to transmission of data
    rest: data, if any
```

or:

```
  word 0: control command
    rest: undefined
```

The general layout of command words is:

```
d15-d12: command identifier
 d11-d8: sequence number modulo 16
  d7-d0: command dependent information
```

except that control commands have no sequence number and the sequence number field is used as an extension to the command identifier.

Assignments of command identifiers are:

```
00000000 null command
0011.... RDY
0101.... NOTRDY
1010.... DATA
1100.... NODATA
01100011 RESET
01100110 CLOSE
   where '....' represents the sequence number.
```

Note that RDY and NOTRDY may only appear in word 0, and DATA and NODATA may only appear in word 1. (This is intended to aid implementation on simple machines.)

If word 1 contains a DATA command, then the packet contains between 0 and 2044 bytes of data. Data starts in word 2 (if present) and goes on until the end of the packet; the more significant byte of each word is the earlier in the byte stream. Four flag bits are defined in the d7-d0 field of the DATA command:

d0: if 1, indicates that the packet contains an odd number of data bytes, and that the less significant byte of the last word should be ignored.
d1: if 1, indicates a request to force transmission of currently buffered data.
d2: if 1, indicates that the byte stream should be closed when the data has been delivered to its eventual destination.
d3: if 1, indicates that the data is control information. This is reserved for future use - in current implementations, such data should be discarded. Bits d1 and d2, if set, should however be acted upon normally.

Note that it is legal to send zero bytes of data (and this is not the same as NODATA). This may be useful if the 'force transmission' or 'close request' is set.

Undefined command dependent information should be kept zero, in order to allow for future expansion.

7 Timeouts

The choice of timeout values will depend on various factors, such as the speed at which machines are able to respond to commands and the required throughput under error conditions. Since the error rate is expected to be low, the latter is not a major factor. A typical timeout value would be one or two seconds. The value of the 'idle handshake' timeout will normally be very much larger - a value of about a minute being typical.

The number of retries to allow before taking more drastic action (RESET, CLOSE or simply abandoning the whole connection) is best determined by experience.

8 Implementation notes

The protocol is designed in such a manner that simple machines can have two fixed buffers, one for transmission and one for reception. On receiving a packet into the reception buffer, the commands it contains may be processed independently, and the appropriate parts of the transmission buffer updated. During this operation, it will be decided whether or not the updated packet should be transmitted or not. This technique may lead to some unnecessary repetition of non-essential elements, but this is defined to be harmless.

If an implementation is subject to real time delays in responding to commands, such that the other party may timeout even when a packet has not been lost, the protocol can lock into a stable state in which every packet is sent twice (or more) and acknowledged a similar number of times. Data is still transferred correctly, but the throughput is reduced. It remains to be seen whether this will turn out to be a problem in practice. Implementations which engage in multiple buffering of input requests will be particularly susceptible to this problem, and may require algorithms to detect and correct this state.

Typical implementations of the byte stream protocol in operating systems run at higher priority than the processes which are supplying or consuming the data. This can lead to $NODATA_n$ and $DATA_n$ frequently being sent in quick succession (similarly $NOTRDY_n$, RDY_n). If the other end of the connection has only one reception buffer, it is quite likely that the latter command will be lost. This leads to frequent pauses in the communication while timeouts expire.

A simple solution to this is to refrain from sending the non-essential element on the transition from 'E' state to 'N' state. (Since the protocol gives protection against the loss of any particular packet, this is guaranteed to be safe.) If a new buffer becomes available in the near future, the next essential element will be transmitted. If on the other hand, the pause in the flow is genuine, the other end of the connection will time out, and the non-essential element will be 'repeated' - in fact it is being sent for the first time.

Implementors should bear in mind that it is desirable for a byte stream to be able to survive ring failures of several seconds duration, such as are caused by a monitor station 'full reset'. It may be advantageous to ignore all transmission errors, and rely totally on the timeout mechanisms.

Annex A: Packet protocol

This section is a revised copy of the document originally issued as a Systems Research Group project note, by R.D.H. Walker.

A packet commences with a header minipacket of the form shown below:

Field A is the binary pattern 1001.
Field B is the type of the packet:

=0: long packet with checksum
=1: long packet with checksum zero
=2: single minipacket carrying data C
=3: reserved for future use

A long packet consists of:

- header minipacket as described above
- route minipacket
- C+1 data minipackets
- checksum minipacket

A route minipacket consists of a 'port number' in the bottom 12 bits, the packet being notionally directed to that port at the destination station. The remaining 4 bits are reserved and should be kept zero.

The C+1 data minipackets conform to the protocol (e.g. byte stream protocol) that is currently agreed to be in use at the port identified in the route minipacket.

The checksum minipacket for type 0 packets consists of a 16-bit end-around carry checksum over the entire packet from the header minipacket up to, and including, the last data minipacket. In type 1 packets, the notional checksum is sent as zero, and checked to be zero.

The intended method of operation for reception is as follows:

1 While a station is totally unable to receive anything, it keeps its select register zero.
2 When a station is potentially capable of receiving input, it sets its select register to 255.
3 It then listens for a valid header minipacket, ignoring anything which is not a valid header.
4 When a valid header has been found, if the station wishes to receive from the station from which the header came, then the receiving station sets its select register to that source, thus rejecting input from any other source.
5 The receiving station must operate either a per-packet timeout or a per-minipacket timeout (or both) in order to recover from a packet being sent shorter than the header minipacket suggested. The timeouts commence with the reception of the header minipacket. If the timeouts expire at any time henceforth, the input thus far accumulated is ignored, and the station is reset to state 2 above, ignoring the incoming packet.
6 The next minipacket after the header is the route minipacket. If interpretation of this minipacket leads the receiver to believe that it cannot receive the remainder of the packet (e.g. specified port not active) then it may reset itself to state 2 above, ignoring the incoming packet.
7 On reaching the end of the packet, the checksum

minipacket is received and checked. If, for type 1 packets, the checksum is incorrect, or for type 2 packets, it is non-zero, then the entire packet may be ignored as if it had never been received.

8 After reception of a packet, the selection register may be restored to 255 if more input is possible, otherwise zero.

9 As an alternative to resetting immediately to state 2 if a partially received packet is to be rejected, the selection register may be set to zero for a short time in an attempt to cause the transmitter to stop sending. The selection may either be for a fixed time, or until the station hardware indicates that a packet has been rejected 'unselected'. If the latter strategy is used, a timeout would also be required.

For transmission:

1 When transmitting the first minipacket (header) of a packet, due allowance must be made for the possibility of the receiving station being busy or unselected owing to it being in the process of receiving a packet from another source. Attempts to transmit the header should be maintained for at least as long as the longest possible packet can take at that reception station. Any other ring error can be regarded as fatal.

2 Having successfully transmitted the first two packets (header and route), allowance may have to be made for certain reception stations to perform certain set up operations for the packet, during which time the station will reject as "busy".

3 After that, the number of busy rejects that may be expected per minipacket should be very low, as the receiver is supposed to be concentrating on one source only. Any other ring error (e.g. unselected) is fatal. It will be necessary for a transmitting station to have a timeout or repeat count on a per-minipacket or a per-packet basis, in order to recover from a reception station crashing in the middle of a packet. A timeout is also necessary to

recover from certain ring errors (such as power off) which result in a minipacket never returning to its sender.

Annex B: Initial connection

This section describes the protocol normally used to establish a BSP connection. It is not part of the specification of BSP itself for two reasons - it does not preclude the setting up of streams by other means, and it may legitimately be used for opening connections using protocols other than BSP.

Initial connection consists of sending a single packet in each direction. These packets are called the OPEN and OPENACK packets. In the following description the originator of the connection, which sends the OPEN, is called P, and the sender of the OPENACK is called Q.

An OPEN packet is directed to a ring service address. This is usually obtained by looking up a text name in the Name Server, and consists of a triple:

- a station number (8 bits)
- a port number (12 bits)
- a function number (16 bits)

An OPEN packet is directed to the station and port given in the ring service address, and has the following format:

word 0: m.s. byte - the bit pattern 01101010
l.s. byte - reserved, should be kept zero
word 1: port number to be used for reply, P_p.
word 2: the function number part of the ring service address
word 3: the number of BSP parameter words, N
4 to N+3: BSP parameters, see below
N+4 on: further parameters

The OPENACK packet is directed to the station from which the OPEN came, and the port number specified in the OPEN. It has the following format:

word 0: m.s. byte - the bit pattern 01100101
l.s. byte - reserved, should be kept zero
word 1: port number for connection, P_Q.
word 2: return code - zero iff successful
word 3: the number of BSP parameter words, N
4 to N+3: BSP parameters, see below
N+4 on: further parameters

The byte stream is set up if and only if the return code is zero. It uses port P_P from Q to P and P_Q from P to Q.

The following BSP parameters are defined in the OPEN packet:

word 4: largest packet that P is prepared to receive, R_P. The default, if this parameter is not present, is 1024.
word 5: largest packet that P will send, S_P. The default is 1024.

The following BSP parameters are defined in the OPENACK:

word 4: the maximum packet size to be used from P to Q. This is the smaller of the largest packet that Q is prepared to receive, R_Q, and S_P from the OPEN.
word 5: the maximum packet size to be used from Q to P. This is the smaller to the largest packet that Q will send, S_Q, and R_P from the OPEN.

The 'packet sizes' mentioned above are expressed in ring minipackets. They refer to the number of packet protocol data minipackets (i.e. they include byte stream protocol packets but exclude the basic packet header, checksum and route minipackets).

The 'further parameters' area of the OPEN and OPENACK packets may be used for application dependent information. This feature should be used with discretion - it is often more appropriate to send such information down the byte stream itself.

If an OPEN times out and is repeated, it is recommended that P should change its port numbers, to ensure that the correct reply is acted upon.

Annex C: Replug

REPLUG is a facility to enable a machine to open a byte stream between two other machines. It is designed as an extension to the basic protocol and may not be found in all implementations.

The machine that wishes to create the connection must have byte streams open to both of the other machines concerned. It issues a REPLUG command to both of them, and expects a CLOSE in reply. The two byte streams are reset to their initial state as defined in the BSP specification, and are then able to communicate with each other.

In the following description, the initiator of the REPLUG is called R, and the other two machines are called P and Q. R is responsible for computing suitable packet sizes for the connection between P and Q, based on the maximum packet sizes previously agreed between P and R, and between Q and R. The maximum packet size for each station may be decreased, but not increased.

The REPLUG command sent to P has the following format:

```
word 0:  m.s. byte - the bit pattern 01101001
         l.s. byte - reserved, should be kept zero
word 1:  m.s. byte - zero
         l.s. byte - station number of Q
word 2:  port number for packets to Q
word 3:  maximum packet size to be used from Q to P
word 4:  maximum packet size to be used from P to Q
```

A complementary packet is sent to Q.

The acknowledgement to a REPLUG is a CLOSE. If the CLOSE is not received within a timeout interval, the REPLUG may be retried in the usual manner.

Bibliography

Birrell, A.D. & Needham, R.M. 1980. 'A Universal File Server'. IEEE Transactions on Software Engineering, New York, SE-6, 5, 450-3.

Dellar, C.N.R. October 1980. 'Removing Backing Store Administration from the CAP Operating System'. SIGOPS Review, New York, 14, 4, 41-9.

Dion, J. October 1980. 'The Cambridge File Server'. SIGOPS Review, New York, 14, 4, 26-35.

Dion, J. 1981. 'Reliable Storage in a Local Network'. Ph.D. Thesis, University of Cambridge. (Available as University of Cambridge Computer Laboratory Technical Report No. 16).

Garnett, N.H. & Needham, R.M. October 1980. 'An Asynchronous Garbage Collector for the Cambridge File Server'. SIGOPS Review, New York, 14, 4, 36-40.

Herbert, A.J. April 1981. 'The User Interface to the Cambridge Distributed System'. Proceedings of the Second International Conference on Distributed Computing, Versailles.

Herbert, A.J. & Needham, R.M. December 1981. 'Sequencing Computation Steps in a Network'. Proceedings of the Eighth Symposium on Operating Systems Principles, Pacific Grove, California.

Hopper, A. 1978. 'Local Area Communications Networks'. Ph.D. Thesis, University of Cambridge. (Available as University of Cambridge Computer Laboratory Technical Report No. 7).

Hopper, A. 1979. 'Local Area Computer Networks', Local Networks and Distributed Office Systems Conference, Northwood, UK: Online Publications Ltd.

Hopper, A. 1980. The Cambridge Ring - A Local Network. Published in 'Advanced Techniques for Microprocessor Systems', edited by F.K. Hanna, published by Peter Peregrinus.

Hopper, A. & Wheeler, D.J. April 1979. 'Maintenance of Ring Communication Systems'. IEEE Transactions on Communications, New York, COM-27, 4, 760-761.

Hopper, A. & Wheeler, D.J. October 1979. 'Binary Routing Networks'. IEEE Transactions on Computers, New York, C-28, 10, 699-703.

Hopper, A. & Wheeler, D.J. To be published. Local Area Networks: the Cambridge Ring. London: Addison-Wesley.

Leslie, I.M. 1981. 'A Master Clock Repeater for the Cambridge Digital Communication Ring'. Proceedings of the IEE, London, 128, E2, 64-6.

Leslie, I.M., Banerjee, R & Love, S.J. May 1981. 'Organisation of Voice Communication on the Cambridge Ring'. Local Networks and Distributed Office Systems Conference, Northwood, UK: Online Publications Ltd.

Mitchell, J.G. & Dion, J. April 1982. 'A Comparison of Two Network-Based File Servers'. Communications of the Association for Computing Machinery, New York, 25, 2, 233-45.

Needham, R.M. January 1979. 'Adding Capability Access to Conventional File Servers'. SIGOPS Review, New York, 13, 1, 3-4.

Needham, R.M. December 1979. 'Systems Aspects of the Cambridge Ring'. Proceedings of the Seventh Symposium on Operating Systems Principles, Pacific Grove, California.

Spratt, E.B. 1980. 'Operational Experiences with a Cambridge Ring Local Area Network in a University Environment'. Computing Laboratory Report No. 3, University of Kent at Canterbury.

Wilkes, M.V. 1975. 'Communication Using a Digital Ring'. Proceedings of the PACNET Conference, Sendai, Japan.

Wilkes, M.V. October 1979. 'The Impact of Wide Band Local Area Communication'. Proceedings of the First International Conference on Distributed Computing Systems, Huntsville, Alabama.

Wilkes, M.V. & Needham, R.M. 1980. 'The Cambridge Model Distributed System'. SIGOPS Review, New York, 14, 1, 21-9.

Wilkes, M.V. & Wheeler, D.J. May 1979. 'The Cambridge Digital Communication Ring'. Local Area Communications Network Symposium, Boston, Mass. (Sponsored by MITRE Corporation and National Bureau of Standards).

In addition to the authors listed above, the following people have made notable contributions to the project:

R. Anderson	C.G. Girling	D.B. Prince
P.J. Bennett	D.W. Huddart	M. Richards
P.T.M. Brooks	M.A. Johnson	M.F. Richardson
V. Claydon	B.J. Knight	S. Temple
D.H. Craft	D.C.J. Matthews	N.W.P. Unwin
S.C. Crawley	M.R.A. Oakley	R.D.H.W. Walker
J.J. Gibbons	N.J. Ody	I.D. Wilson

Index